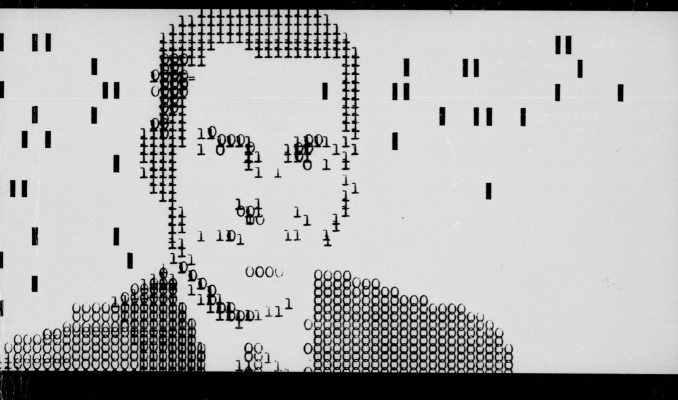

DEVELOPING COMPUTER-BASED EMPLOYEE INFORMATION SYSTEMS

EDWARD J. MORRISON

DEVELOPING COMPUTER-BASED EMPLOYEE INFORMATION SYSTEMS

DEVELOPING COMPUTER-BASED EMPLOYEE INFORMATION SYSTEMS

Edward J. Morrison

AMERICAN MANAGEMENT ASSOCIATION, INC.

This Research Study has been distributed without charge to AMA members enrolled in the Personnel Division.

Standard book number: 8144–3099–6
Library of Congress catalog card number: 72–93020

About This Report

In ELECTRONIC DATA PROCESSING'S FORMATIVE YEARS, MANY COMPANIES APPLIED COMputers initially to repetitive, large-volume clerical tasks and to reports of data vital to the business. Early attention was given to accounting, inventory control, and sales reports, for example. At that time the only extensive use of EDP in the personnel area was for payroll calculations.

As companies progressively put more and more of their reporting systems on computers, they began to look at possibilities of improving services and effectiveness in some of the functions they had first bypassed, such as purchasing, distribution, and personnel. The development of personnel applications was further stimulated by external events. Increasing government regulations regarding employment, manpower shortages in some areas and surpluses in others, spiraling wages and salaries, added complexities of benefit plans, and other factors made companies far more sensitive to personnel problems and to a need for readily accessible, up-to-date employee information. The result was that a growing number of companies began to take a fresh look at their personnel files and reporting systems. Many found that their personnel data were scattered throughout the company, uncoordinated and updated only sporadically.

To improve this situation, companies began to consolidate and computerize payroll-related data and then started moving into the development of programs for descriptive information, work history, and employee job status. Although they usually underestimated the extent and difficulty of these tasks, many discovered major advantages in having computer-based personnel data. They found that they could do more, quantitatively and qualitatively, with EDP personnel systems than they could with their previous systems.

The present report describes the various stages of designing and introducing computer systems by which companies collect, manipulate, and report several types of personnel data. It examines a number of the key factors that need to be considered—such as selection criteria, goals, and priorities—as well as the interrelationships between the various files. The study stresses that even more important than relationships between files are the relationships between people. Conflicts regarding departmental or divisional requirements can seriously impede developmental efforts. The interest and involvement of top executives help create and maintain a suitable climate for effective efforts. Obviously, the large expenditure of funds required makes it imperative that these men be involved during the early stages of systems development. During the later stages their informational needs and their concerns should continue to be a major influence.

To insure the success of computer-based employee information systems, companies have to consider numerous other factors: types of systems, organizational levels to be served, individual users, timing with which a system is to be introduced, translation of systems requirements, preparation of operational procedures, staffing and training of people who will operate the systems, and subsequent supervision of these people. Monitoring procedures have to be established and other steps taken to insure system effectiveness. All these activities are shaped and influenced by a number of organizational and management factors, such as company size, extent of decentralization, corporate policies, type of management, cost orientation, and attitudes regarding innovation.

EDWARD J. MORRISON, who conducted the research and prepared this report, is associate professor of management at the University of Colorado. Dr. Morrison received his D.B.A. from Indiana University in 1959 and has taught organization theory, management fundamentals, personnel management, and labor relations. From 1963 to 1965 he was a senior management engineer in a large aerospace organization, where he worked primarily in the design and implementation of computer-based management information systems. He is also a consultant to business, government, and research organizations.

Publications by Dr. Morrison include several articles for business and management publications, such as *The California Management Review* and the *Journal of Marketing,* and a monograph, "The Nature and Role of the Management Process." A native of West Virginia, he is a member of several professional and honorary organizations, including the Academy of Management, Alpha Kappa Psi, Sigma Iota Epsilon, and Beta Gamma Sigma.

Thanks are extended to the University of Colorado Council on Research and Creative Work for providing computer and clerical assistance and other support for the project. The author expresses appreciation to John Dobel and John Hubbs, two former graduate students at the university, for conducting computer analysis of the questionnaire data and for providing data-bank analysis. He also acknowledges with thanks the guidance and assistance of Margaret Higginson, AMA senior research associate, and the copy editing of Roberta Pavlu, AMA research study editor.

JOHN W. ENELL
Vice President for Research

Contents

Exhibits

Appendixes

1. Patterns of EDP Applications in Personnel

COMPUTERS HAVE BEEN EStablished as a valuable tool for accounting, inventory, customer billing, production, and payroll, but personnel applications are a somewhat shaded area. Many people are looking at 'people information' to see what can be done to take the shade off." This statement by Philip Morgan, vice president of Information Science Incorporated, reflects a typical attitude toward the application of computers and advanced information technology to personnel information in businesses across the country.

A few years ago there was relatively little interest in EDP applications for the personnel function. Today many companies are using EDP to process personnel information to cut administrative costs, to gain greater knowledge about the quality of their workforces, and to permit better utilization of their human resources.

Because of companies' increased interest in using computers for processing personnel information, the present survey was conducted to determine the extent and nature of EDP application for this purpose. Widespread interest in EDP applications in the personnel function was indicated by the large number of responses—45 percent of the 900 companies contacted. Moreover, two-thirds of the respondents reported that they now have some computerized personnel applications in addition to payroll-data processing. Sophistication of these applications varies widely; some firms have highly developed computer programs in almost all phases of their personnel functions while other companies have EDP applications that provide only a modicum of payroll data.

Computer Use in Personnel and Other Functions

The responding companies reported using computers more for processing payroll data than for any other type of application. Other areas of heavy concentration are accounting, sales, and inventory. The following is a breakdown of the EDP applications in use by the 408 respondents:

Application	No. of Companies	Percent
Payroll	363	89
Accounting	347	85
Sales	309	76
Inventory	303	74
Personnel	271	67
Billing	268	66
Production	247	61
Finance	211	52
Engineering	135	33
Purchasing	122	30
Other	52	13

That more companies report the use of computers for personnel than for billing and finance may be because most of the questionnaires were completed by personnel executives or by managers of systems functions who are interested in personnel applications. Moreover, these data indicate only the number of personnel applications, not the percentage of time utilized on company computers or the degree of sophistication of applications. Nevertheless, the author believes that the prevalence of personnel applications is significant.

9

EXHIBIT 1. *Computer-Based Personnel Applications in Participating Companies of Varying Size*

	COMPANIES WITH FEWER THAN 1,000 EMPLOYEES	COMPANIES WITH 1,000–5,000 EMPLOYEES	COMPANIES WITH MORE THAN 5,000 EMPLOYEES	ALL COMPANIES
	(N=61)	(N=155)	(N=192)	(N=408)
	Percent	*Percent*	*Percent*	*Percent*
Nonpayroll-Related Personnel Applications	18	25	57	39
Payroll-Related Personnel Applications	30	33	22	28
No Present Personnel Applications–Plans Only	11	22	13	16
No Present Personnel Applications–No Plans	41	20	8	17

Obviously, there is a strong relationship between payroll and personnel applications in a company. Some personnel applications are totally dependent upon payroll data—that is, information such as deductions for insurance, profit-sharing data, and pension plan payments are part of the information used in calculating net payroll—or they pertain to other financial and accounting records normally processed with the payroll. These data may also be used by the personnel department for administering personnel programs.

Ninety percent of the responding companies that have or plan to have payroll applications also have or plan to have personnel applications. Only 1 percent of the companies (5 out of 408 respondents) report EDP applications in personnel but no payroll applications, and all these firms plan to put payroll data on the computer in the near future.

Approximately 28 percent (112) of the respondents have only payroll-related personnel applications. Thirty-nine percent of them (159) report additional personnel applications that are unrelated to payroll

data, such as skills inventories, medical data, and job evaluation data. Sixteen percent (66) report that, while they do not presently have any computer applications in personnel, they plan to develop these applications within the next five years. (See Exhibit 1.)

The amount of time the 66 respondents estimated that they would require to develop EDP applications is as follows.

1 year .... 17 companies
2 years .... 30 companies
3 years .... 12 companies
4–5 years .... 7 companies

While 17 percent (71) of the responding companies report that they neither have nor plan to develop computer applications in personnel, 8 percent (32) of the responding companies neither have nor plan to develop computer applications in payroll. These questionnaire data are consistent with interview data gathered during this research since they indicate that payroll and personnel data are natural adjuncts. If a computerized application exists in one area, an application in the other area is likely to follow.

Present and Planned
Personnel Applications

In a manual data system personnel records often are maintained by the employment department or kept in a separate employee records section. Other parts of personnel data are functionally oriented— that is, they are kept by the functional section that has responsibility for the work to which the data pertain. Often there is little agreement among these various data files. If payroll is a separate organizational function, payroll data often are collected, processed, and reported quite independently of

---

BASIS OF THE RESEARCH

The author obtained the information for this study from depth interviews and a questionnaire survey sample drawn from the 1967 edition of *Poor's Register of Corporations, Directors, and Executives*. A disproportional stratified sampling approach was used to select 900 companies at random: 300 firms with 500 to 999 employees, 300 with 1,000 to 4,999 employees, and 300 with more than 5,000 employees. A number of these companies are U.S. fabricating and processing firms; the remainder are transportation companies, financial institutions, utilities companies, and other types of organizations.

The questionnaire, previously developed and field-tested in a survey among Colorado companies, was mailed in June 1967 to the top personnel executive in the 900 firms. Over 45 percent (408) of the companies responded. The number of responses within the three size categories was as follows:

No. of Employees	No. of Companies
500–999	61
1,000–4,999	155
5,000 or more	192

During the summer of 1967, the author visited 18 companies to conduct a number of depth interviews, some lasting several days. He talked with top personnel executives; systems analysts, programmers, and personnel information specialists who had developed personnel data systems; and users of these systems. Among the companies that participated in these interviews were Eastman Kodak Company, Ford Motor Company, Honeywell Inc., International Business Machines Corporation, Eli Lilly and Company, McDonnell Douglas Corporation, Mobil Oil Company, Polaroid Corporation, Radio Corporation of America, Standard Oil Company (Ohio), U.S. Plywood-Champion Papers Inc., Walker Manufacturing Company, and Xerox Corporation. These companies were selected for study because they had been using advanced computer-based personnel systems from two to ten years. The author analyzed computer layouts of personnel data banks in seven of these companies. He also visited and interviewed executives at two firms specializing in computer systems—Information Science Incorporated and Time Share Corporation.

Participating companies have consented to the publication of all quotations, descriptions of activities, and exhibit materials in this report. While the author was obtaining permissions, he verified that the participants were still using the computer-based personnel systems described.

Personnel activities. In many cases the payroll department is reluctant to supply wage and salary information to the personnel department.

As a company develops a computer-based employee information system, the lines between separate data banks begin to fade. Some companies eventually have a single data bank for all "people data." This data bank is usually fed by only a few input documents, but is designed to perform the work of several payroll, accounting, and personnel functions, and uses a number of computer programs. Data are collected in a single base, and information is reported out of the base as needed.

Most of the companies studied have personnel files that are somewhere between a manual system and a single computer data bank for all personnel information. A majority of the companies have more than one personnel base, and all have some special-purpose data files that serve specific functional activities. Not one company reports having a completely integrated employee information system.

While the survey questionnaire was designed to obtain information about functional activities, the interviews focused upon actual data-base arrangements, which are not neatly divisible along functional lines. Therefore, statements from the two sources sometimes seem unrelated, but in general they are complementary and are presented simultaneously.

MAJOR AREAS OF APPLICATION

Four general classifications of data are discernible from this study. The first category is *payroll data,* which includes those items necessary to calculate gross payroll and gross-to-net payroll, such as employee name, pay rate, account number, time worked, shift code, and insurance, withhold-ing tax, and other deductions. The second category of information, *payroll-related data,* includes pension data, workmen's compensation information, date of hire, profit-sharing figures, sales to employees, and wage and salary records.

The third category is *descriptive information;* it comprises age, sex, marital status, home address, telephone number, military status, and other such items of information about an employee. This category of data may also include skills-inventory information, which describes an employee's skills and abilities, his work preferences, and other items of information that indicate his potential value to a company. The fourth category of information is *job status and work history.* In this category are such items as work location, job title, department number, job-classification information, labor grade, and other data that identify where an employee is in a company and what he is doing there. The work history shows what an employee has done in the past and keeps a running record of his various positions in the company over a period of time. Items in each of these four categories are not necessarily kept in separate files. Often there is overlap and duplication among various data files.

In developing an employee information system, companies usually put payroll data on the computer first. They may also include some payroll-related information that is to be reported to Personnel during the early stage. The next step may be in either of two directions: Some firms put descriptive data in the computer-based files for the purposes of describing what types of people they have in the company and what these people can do. Other firms are more concerned with "statusing" the workforce and concentrate on job status and work history information in an effort to determine exactly where everyone is and what he is doing. The types of data a company

EXHIBIT 2. *Companies with One or More EDP Applications—Present or Planned—in Each Major Personnel Function*

(N=408)

	NO. OF COMPANIES WITH APPLICATIONS	NO. OF COMPANIES PLANNING APPLICATIONS	TOTAL NO. OF COMPANIES	TOTAL PERCENT OF COMPANIES
Employee Services	233	74	307	75
Employment & Staffing	177	119	296	73
Wage & Salary Administration	184	90	274	67
Labor Relations	172	99	271	66
Personnel Research	95	127	222	54
Health & Safety	85	104	189	46
Training & Education	42	108	150	37

chooses to gather, process, and report depend primarily on its specific needs at a given time and the amount of pressure that is exerted to have these needs met. This development is discussed in greater detail in Chapter 3, which describes the whole process by which companies develop an employee information system.

Which activities within the personnel department make the most use of computerized data? Exhibit 2 shows the number of respondents reporting EDP applications in one or more activities within each of the major functions of personnel. Other than payroll, the most common area in which firms use computer-processed information is employee services, primarily because of the need for insurance and pension data. Wage and salary administration is second in the list of functions most active in using computerized data. As in the case of employee-services data, wage and salary information is payroll-related. Also prevalent are computerized data used for determining the status of the workforce; that is, for employment and staffing and labor relations. Those functions that deal primarily with descriptive data—namely, health, safety, training, and education—use computerized data least.

When computerized information is classified according to the functional activities that are served, certain patterns emerge that give a clue to the major interests of the reporting companies. Of the present applications, shown in Exhibit 3, payroll-related data and data concerned with status of the workforce are the most prevalent. Almost half the companies have pension and insurance data on computers. But only about 15 percent (60) have computerized skills-inventory data, and less than 10 percent have other types of descriptive data on computers. By contrast, nearly 44 percent (178) of the respondents are planning to computerize skills-inventory data, and approximately 30 percent are planning applications in turnover, manpower forecasts, employment records, promotions, and transfers. A number of respondents plan to put on computers other types of data relating to status, as well as descriptive and payroll-related data. (See Exhibit 4.)

While activities relating to compensation receive top priority in computer applications, companies are also very concerned with the nature and status of their workforces. Status-related activities seem to be more important to companies than those that deal with description—with the exception of skills inventory—but even the latter are being provided with computer-processed information by an increasing number of companies.

EXHIBIT 3. *Present EDP Applications of Personnel Data, in Ranked Order*

(N=408)

PAYROLL-RELATED	STATUS OF WORKFORCE	DESCRIPTIVE DATA	PROGRAM AND OTHER	NUMBER OF COMPANIES	PERCENT
Payroll				363	88.9
Pensions				196	48.0
Insurance				195	47.8
Wage & Salary Records				155	38.0
	Employment & Staffing Records			139	34.1
	Seniority			136	33.3
Profit Sharing				91	22.3
	Separations			90	22.1
Wage & Salary Surveys				90	22.1
	Transfers			83	20.3
			Statistical Studies	80	19.6
	Absenteeism			73	17.9
	Promotions			70	17.2
	Turnover			63	15.4
		Skills Inventory		60	14.7
Wage & Salary Structure				58	14.2
Workmen's Compensation				51	12.5
	Layoff			51	12.5
Sales to Employees				50	12.3
Credit Union				48	11.8
	Turnover Studies			45	11.0
	Separation Studies			43	10.5
			Job Evaluation	39	9.6
		Training & Ed. Records		36	8.8
	Manpower Forecasts			35	8.6
	Manning Studies			32	7.8
		Accident Data		32	7.8

Exhibit 3 (*continued*)

PAYROLL-RELATED	STATUS OF WORKFORCE	DESCRIPTIVE DATA	PROGRAM AND OTHER	NUMBER OF COMPANIES	PERCENT
		Medical Records		29	7.1
		Health & Safety Records		29	7.1
			Labor Contract Data	24	5.9
	Selection			23	5.6
	Promotion Studies			23	5.6
			Job Descriptions	23	5.6
	Recruitment			20	4.9
			Health Programs	15	3.7
		Man Specifications		14	3.4
			Misc. Employee Services	12	2.9
			Safety Programs	12	2.9
			Training & Ed. Evaluation	12	2.9
Misc. Wage & Salary				10	2.5
			Training Programs	8	2.0
	Misc. Employment & Staffing			4	1.0
			Personnel Policies	4	1.0
			Suggestions	3	0.7
			Grievances	2	0.5
			Misc. Labor Relations	2	0.5
			Retraining Studies	2	0.5
			Misc. Training & Ed.	1	0.2
			Misc. Health & Safety	1	0.2

Of course, the data in the exhibits can be interpreted differently. For example, skills inventory may be considered an activity concerned with status rather than with description since it facilitates the movement of skills from one location to another. While reclassification might develop a clearer picture of the applications being implemented and planned by responding companies, the overall picture would be altered very little.

SIZE AND SOPHISTICATION

As might be expected, computer-based personnel applications in small firms are usually less sophisticated than they are in larger companies. Also, large firms are more likely to have a greater number of active, nonpayroll-related personnel applications. However, examination of individual questionnaires and interviews with companies of various sizes indicates that the number

EXHIBIT 4. *Planned EDP Applications of Personnel Data, in Ranked Order*

(N=408)

PAYROLL-RELATED	STATUS OF WORKFORCE	DESCRIPTIVE DATA	PROGRAM AND OTHER	NUMBER OF COMPANIES	PERCENT
		Skills Inventory		178	43.6
	Labor Turnover			134	32.8
	Manpower Forecasts			130	31.9
	Turnover Studies			129	31.6
	Employment & Staffing			119	29.2
	Promotions			118	28.9
	Transfers			111	27.2
	Manning Studies			111	27.2
			Statistical Studies	108	26.5
	Absenteeism			107	26.2
	Separation Studies			106	26.0
		Accident Data		101	24.8
	Separations			97	23.8
		Training & Ed. Records		94	23.0
	Selection			92	22.5
Wage & Salary Surveys				92	22.5
	Promotion Studies			92	22.5
	Layoff			88	21.6
				87	21.3
Insurance				85	20.8
Wage & Salary Records				82	20.1
	Recruitment		Training & Ed. Evaluation	81	19.9
		Medical Data		78	19.1
Workmen's Compensation				75	18.4
Pensions				75	18.4
		Health & Safety Records		74	18.1
	Seniority			73	17.9

EXHIBIT 4 *(continued)*

PAYROLL-RELATED	STATUS OF WORKFORCE	DESCRIPTIVE DATA	PROGRAM AND OTHER	NUMBER OF COMPANIES	PERCENT
Payroll (Part or Total)				71	17.4
		Man Specifications		64	15.7
			Training Programs	62	15.2
Wage & Salary Structure				61	15.0
			Retraining Studies	57	14.0
			Safety Programs	55	13.5
			Job Evaluation	54	13.2
			Contract Data	53	13.0
			Grievances	47	11.5
			Health Programs	46	11.3
			Job Descriptions	41	10.0
Profit Sharing				30	7.4
			Suggestions	30	7.4
			Personnel Policies	24	5.9
Sales to Employees				21	5.1
Credit Union				17	4.2
Misc. Wage & Salary				4	1.0
	Misc. Employment & Staffing			3	0.7
			Misc. Employee Services	2	0.5
			Misc. Health & Safety	2	0.5
			Misc. Training & Ed.	2	0.5
			Misc. Labor Relations	1	0.2

of personnel applications is not necessarily related to company size. Also, there seems to be no direct relationship between the size of company and the degree of sophistication of its computer-based personnel applications. Furthermore, the number of personnel applications a company has on the computer does not necessarily indicate sophistication. The extent of variation in the personnel applications of respondents and the relationship between company size and the degree of sophistication of personnel applications will be discussed more fully in later chapters.

In an effort to determine what is being done by relatively sophisticated companies, the author selected 15 of them for intensive interviews. Three others were interviewed less intensively. The length of time that these firms had computer applications in personnel ranged from two to ten years. Interviews were conducted with personnel executives, managers of systems departments, and top executives to whom the chief personnel executives and systems managers reported, as well as personnel, systems, and line people who had knowledge and experience in developing and working with employee information systems. These interviews confirmed the existence of a wide variation in sophistication.

Most of the present computer applications in personnel are oriented toward administration and control of the personnel function. Some firms have provided only enough capacity to produce a few reports in a fixed format during the processing of their payroll files. Other companies have created very complex systems that are using a number of integrated modules of various kinds of personnel and payroll data, and have the capacity to interrelate these files mechanically through the computer. A few firms have developed management-science types of applications, such as computerized models for policy simulation and for prediction of personnel trends. But this latter type of application is relatively uncommon.

Determining Patterns

The purpose of this research was twofold: (1) to find out what EDP applications are being made by companies for their personnel functions and (2) to develop a rationale for their use of these applications.

It was hoped that the questionnaire survey of 900 companies would reveal a discernible pattern of specific EDP applications in personnel activities. Other than the patterns previously mentioned in this chapter, this hope was not realized. The author postulated that there might be some logical starting place for companies that

wish to apply computers to their employee information handling problems. He further postulated that there might possibly be a logical sequence for adding other applications. He thought that firms with only a few applications might have the same types of applications and that several firms having many applications also might have approximately the same applications. However, the results did not produce any discernible patterns.

In addition to analyzing the questionnaire responses, the author analyzed computer-tape layouts of data banks in seven companies. He discovered that firms of the same size do not have the same size data bank—the banks range from 200 to over 5,000 characters of information—and that data banks of approximately the same size do not contain the same data elements. Again, no consistent pattern of applications emerged.

A third source of information was the interviews. In conducting them, the author found more differences than similarities among the answers to his questions. The types of applications used seemed to depend more on the problems to be solved and the individual company's approach to their solution than on any consistent, logical pattern of handling employee information. Reflecting this problem-orientation, members of management seem to identify pressing personnel problems and develop an employee information system to help solve those specific problems.

In the study of computer applications, whether one follows a textbook definition of personnel functions and activities, or uses an empirical approach, or examines the elements in various data banks, there seems to be no discernible pattern of applications in the personnel function.

When this research was initiated, the author formulated several questions to guide his efforts. While he was conducting the project, some of these questions proved to be sound and others seemed rather naïve or inconsequential. A review of a few of these early questions helps put the research into perspective.

• *Does organizational size, structure, or type of business have an effect on EDP applications in the personnel function?* No clearcut patterns of applications are apparent among the various companies that participated in this study. As mentioned previously, the number and sophistication of EDP applications in personnel were not directly related to the size or type of business studied. The scope and use of computers in handling personnel information seem to be more related to factors such as top management philosophy and expertise in information technology in the specific companies and personnel departments. Although the attitudes and abilities needed to develop complex employee information systems are more likely to be found in larger companies—as are the financial resources necessary to support the expense of designing and implementing such a system —there is no direct or necessary correlation between size or type of company and the development of sophisticated information systems.

• *What is the relationship between EDP applications in personnel and EDP applications in other functions in a company?* No company interviewed or surveyed indicated that personnel was the first or the foremost computer application. Personnel applications are integrally tied to payroll applications, and payroll was generally an earlier, more prestigious application. The cost of acquiring a computer and the main support of computer facilities are borne by other functional areas of a company.

• *How do firms evaluate their computer-based personnel applications?* In general, companies indicate that EDP personnel applications permit them to provide more personnel services of a better quality, with no increase in the number of people required in the personnel department. Very few firms report a cost saving as a result of the transition from manual to computer processing of employee information. A majority of companies intend to increase their use of computers in the personnel function.

Some people contend that personnel is only dabbling in the field of computer applications, that such applications are not absolutely necessary, and that they serve primarily as a status symbol. In the opinion of the author, most companies are genuinely concerned about their need to apply information technology to solve their personnel problems. Many of these firms are trying to make the information acquired from personnel applications useful for management decision making. However, few of them are attempting full integration of information concerning human resources with information regarding their other resources—that is, none of the firms studied has a completely integrated management information system. In the few companies that are making such attempts, personnel information seems to be on the outermost fringe.

• *How do companies design and implement employee information systems?* Personnel people, systems specialists, and line groups are involved in designing and implementing employee information systems. In some companies this process is directed primarily by the personnel department; in others systems specialists play the major role. Those firms in which personnel took a strong, competent role in this process generally are more satisfied with the results of their efforts than are companies in which systems assumed the stronger role. In general, companies reported that they are surprised about the cost, time, and effort involved in designing and implementing employee information systems. Because the complexity of the problems and processes involved is not always readily apparent, it is easy to underestimate the extent and difficulty of the job.

Companies that have worked for several years in applying computers and advanced information technology to personnel data have much practical advice to impart to novices in this endeavor. Therefore, this report describes the rationale for developing EDP applications in personnel expressed by executives and managers in the 18 companies selected for interviews. Rather than trying to condense the companies' experiences into a single, consistent pattern for developing an employee information system, the study reports the major determinants and reasons for each firm's efforts to develop an employee information system to meet its needs at a specific time.

As previously noted, most companies have employee information systems that are concerned primarily with administering the function. A few firms are developing management-science applications in personnel, such as models for simulation and prediction. Personnel executives report a great need to develop computer applications that will permit the computer to handle routine personnel information processing to release personnel managers for activities more germane to management. Executives also report a need for information about human resources for management decision making that can be gathered, processed, and reported by computer-based employee information systems. Newer techniques of management science and advanced information technology, such as "demand information" and optical display devices, eventually will permit more effective management use of personnel information.

"Computers will change organizational roles and structure," states Glen Galles, manager of personnel research of Honeywell, Inc. "Management will no longer have to supervise its own paperwork, and therefore will have more time for making decisions and planning." He further states, "Although the computer is often overrated and given a mystic air, it does change the nature of the information process—quantitatively, qualitatively, and through time (immediacy); thus organizations are likely to change to reflect this new capacity."

The advent of computers does not necessarily demand or dictate a change in the organization of the personnel department, or in the way the function is managed, but it certainly does invite change. Certainly, it makes new demands on the management of the personnel function.

CHANGES RESULTING FROM APPLICATIONS

The companies surveyed by questionnaire were asked to identify changes resulting from the use of computers for their personnel information systems. Over 80 percent (188) of 233 respondents report that the number of employees in their personnel departments has not changed, and over half (117) of 219 firms that the cost of their personnel services has not changed. Over 60 percent (140) of 231 companies indicate that the number of personnel services they offer has increased, and two-thirds (156) that the quality of services offered by the personnel department has increased. Only one-fifth (46) of the firms report a cost savings; and one-tenth (23), a reduction in personnel employees. (See Exhibit 5.)

These questionnaire data are fairly consistent with the interview data collected during the study. Very few of the companies interviewed had reduced their costs or the number of people employed in their personnel departments. Most of them emphasized that they could do considerably more, both qualitatively and quantitatively, in handling their personnel data with computer applications.

EXHIBIT 5. *Changes in Personnel Services and Number of Personnel Employees Resulting from EDP*

| | INCREASE | | DECREASE | | NO CHANGE | | |
TYPE OF CHANGE	NO. OF COMPANIES	PERCENT	NO. OF COMPANIES	PERCENT	NO. OF COMPANIES	PERCENT	TOTAL NUMBER
Quality of Services Offered by Personnel	156	68	7	3	67	29	230
Number of Services Offered by Personnel	140	61	2	1	88	38	231
Cost of Personnel Services	57	26	46	21	117	53	219
Number of Employees in Personnel Department	21	9	23	10	188	81	233

EXHIBIT 6. *Degree of Satisfaction with Personnel Applications in Companies of Varying Size*

(N=233)

Size of Company	HIGHLY SATISFIED Percent	MODERATELY SATISFIED Percent	VERY LITTLE SATISFACTION Percent	NOT SATISFIED Percent	NO. OF COMPANIES
Under 1,000 Employees	16	72	12	—	25
1,000–5,000 Employees	36	56	5	3	80
Over 5,000 Employees	33	57	7	3	128
All Companies	32	58	7	3	233

SATISFACTION WITH APPLICATIONS

How satisfied are companies with the results of their efforts to use computers for processing personnel data? Almost one-third (75) of the 233 respondents report that they are highly satisfied; 58 percent (135) say that they are moderately satisfied; and 10 percent (23) report very little or no satisfaction with results. These findings are relatively consistent, regardless of the size of the company reporting. (See Exhibit 6.)

Although no statistical correlations were attempted between the data obtained from questionnaires and interviews, they seemed to indicate the same pattern. Executives in several companies of varying size expressed great satisfaction with their computer-based employee information systems, while executives in most companies cited reasons for some discontent with specific parts of their information systems. Very few executives have strongly negative attitudes toward EDP applications that have been in operation for an extended period of time.

Of 408 responding companies, only 9 report that they have discontinued specific EDP applications in personnel. Four firms report that they have given up their attempts to maintain a skills inventory. Some of the reasons cited were problems of updating and coding information, need for a different or less complex system, and unsatisfactory results. Two companies had discontinued their applications covering medical data; at the same time one of them had also discontinued its applications in health and safety records and accident data. The first company reports that it could not justify the cost of collecting the input data, and the other indicates that the medical data simply were not used.

One company reports that its payroll operations were "farmed out" to an outside agency when the division gave up its computer. Another firm dropped an EDP application in seniority because it had so few employees—under 350—that the cost of maintaining the system made it impractical.

Still another firm reports giving up the attempt to maintain its personnel records on the computer because of inability to keep the records current. But one of its executives commented, "We're now trying again." These nine companies represent only 3 percent of those firms that have EDP applications in personnel. All but one company have other types of computer applications that are being continued. It may be concluded that these abortive attempts were more or less isolated and reflect unusual circumstances rather than a general situation among companies with personnel applications.

2. The Nature and Scope of Employee Information Systems

When a company decides to design and implement a computer-based system to collect, store, process, and report information about its employees, many critical decisions are made about who should be included in the data files and how much information is needed on each individual. Decisions are also made about the most desirable methods of collecting and auditing data and manipulating various employee data files. Personnel and systems people decide on file structure and the system for inputting and editing data, as well as what information is to be reported out of the files and how this is to be accomplished.

The interrelationships among various files of employee information and other related resource data are then established. These decisions entail an understanding of departmental needs and value systems that determine the nature and use of employee information within the company. Of particular importance is the relationship between the personnel files and the payroll data files.

The nature and scope of a particular company's employee information system depend upon the decisions made by line management, personnel people, and systems specialists during the design and implementation stages. In many ways the system will mirror the methods typically used by the company to manage its human resources. So that the relationship between the system as a management tool and the company's typical methods of using information and managing human resources can be seen clearly, it would be helpful to review some of the characteristics of employee information systems and the management decisions that are implicit in the design and implementation of such systems.

What Are Systems?

One of the most overworked words in business is "system." Another term used extensively is "management information system." Although these terms are given a variety of specific meanings by authorities in the systems field, their use in this report will conform more to the loose definitions applied in business today. "System" will refer to a group of related elements that have some common properties, interacting functions, and mutual relationships, while "management information system" will refer to a system that provides members of management with the information about a company's ongoing activities that they need to make sound decisions. An *employee information system* accepts inputs of data about employees; it processes, stores, and manipulates these data; and it provides outputs, or reports, of such information for the performance and management of personnel activities in a company.

Alternative titles for employee information system that are used in business today include "industrial relations information system," "employee relations information system," "personnel information system," and "personnel data system." In general, these systems are concerned with what management calls, for want of a better term, "people information"—any information that relates to, describes, or reflects people and what they do in an organization. As defined by Philip Morgan, vice president of Information Science Incorporated, an employee information system is "a systematic technique of data handling that organizes, maintains, and reports employee information, using electronic data processing (EDP) to meet information needs of top management, the personnel function, and employees." According to Mr. Morgan, an employee information system (1) facilitates the performance of regular personnel function activities, (2) provides management with information for decision making, and (3) also may serve employee needs directly.

NOT ALL SYSTEMS ARE ALIKE

A cursory glance at present applications in personnel will show that the variations among employee information systems are almost infinite. Robert V. Syrett, of the accounting and information services department, Esso Mathematics and Systems, Inc., states: "Getting computerized in personnel may be analogous to buying accounting equipment. You can have very large scale applications or small-scale applications. You can have sophisticated software, or a pocket-size program. It all depends on your size and your specific needs."

Configurations vary tremendously among firms and, of course, not all are computer-based. As mentioned previously, they reflect the mood and mode of management. For example, a company's information technology might take any of the following approaches:

- Manual operations, with little or no attempt to employ systems concepts.

- Rather thoroughly worked out manual systems.
- EAM-based (electronic accounting machine) information processing.
- Computer-based processing in which the computer is used primarily as a file and a "large typewriter."
- Computer-based systems that use the computer as a tool to audit personnel activities against established policies and goals and to process information (serving as a logic device).
- Computer-based systems, with the primary function of serving management decision making, possibly having the capacity for 24-hour turnaround from question to answer.
- Advanced computer-based systems, with demand-information capability, instant updating of individual records from remote terminals, exception reporting on a broad scale, and management-science applications.

While this is only a partial list of configurations, it gives some idea of the various types of employee information systems used by the firms interviewed in this study.

SYSTEMS-DESIGN CONSIDERATIONS

In defining their needs for information, and assessing priorities for approaching the design of a computer-based employee information system, personnel managers report that they must have answers to a number of fundamental questions. These include the following:

1. About whom should information be included in the system?
   Should it include everyone in the organization?
   Should all salary classes be included? All hourly employees?

Should all plants and subsidiaries, and all functions at each location, be included?

2. How much data should be kept about each person?

   Should the same data be kept about all persons?

   Should the data be gathered and entered into the system all at once?

3. Will employee work history be collected and stored?

   How far back should one go in collecting data on work history: One year? Five years? From each employee's date of accession?

   How much data on different types of work will be kept about an employee? What kinds of data are significant?

4. How will basic data be collected initially, and how will they be routinely changed?

   Will old, manually kept records be used to capture initial inputs, or will a one-shot input from each source be used?

   How will initial inputs be edited and audited?

   What method of changing data will be used? Will regular reports generate changes, or will there be a one-shot, once-a-year change?

5. Will the basic data-reporting document, such as an employee-change notice, also be used as a record by local personnel managers?

6. Will routine audits of data be made manually or by machine? Will they be made at regular intervals?

   During normal file maintenance and updating, will input audits be made?

   Will the computer be used to audit and enforce personnel policies and objectives?

7. What will be the relationships among the files and parts of the system?

Will files be separate and more or less unrelated? Related by the use of common coding systems and data-element definition? Related by the capability to machine cross-check various files, which insures the commonality of people and data in each? Integrated to permit maintenance of one file with data from another and to have report generation drawing data from more than one file for incorporation in a single report?

8. Specifically, what will be the relationship between personnel files and payroll files?

9. What personnel functions will be served? The possibilities include personnel records, wage and salary administration, training, recruitment and employment, management development, appraisal, employee services, health and safety, labor reporting, absence control, vacation scheduling, and personnel research. In what order will each of these applications be implemented?

10. What kind of management information reporting is desirable? The range may include the following:

    Simple routine tabular reports.

    Reports produced routinely during file maintenance.

    Special reports generated by adding control cards during file maintenance.

    Reports requiring special programming or generated by nonprogrammers who access file information.

    Reports through special mathematical capability, such as accumulators or complex mathematical analyses.

11. Will the system be used primarily for administration and control of rou-

tine activities; primarily for short-range management decision making; or will the system also include some capability for use in long-range planning and personnel research in which it is characterized by management-science applications?

In sum, companies that are designing employee information systems are concerned with four major factors:

1. How much and what kind of data will be collected and processed on which people in the organization?
2. How will these data be collected, edited, manipulated, and stored?
3. How will data be reported out of the system?
4. What will be the interrelationships among various files containing information about people in the organization?

The remainder of this chapter will attempt to answer these questions.

Data Selection

A number of companies that were visited indicated that they were a little too ambitious when they first decided to convert to machine processing of personnel data. Most managers admitted that they would have been better off scaling down their original grandiose plans. They commented that a natural beginning was to ask: "What would we like to know about people?" and to decide that they wanted to include everything. But the companies soon found that their lists became much too long. Although their initial questions seemed reasonable at first and their goals laudable, they found that the task of developing an employee information system is large enough to challenge the skill, if not the imagination, of most personnel executives.

Any firm wishing to develop a computer-based employee information system finds, among its needs and aspirations, the need to establish clearcut goals and priorities related to its proposed budget and abilities. Developing a complete information system is a time-consuming and money-consuming process, but the potential rewards are great.

"One of EDP's biggest advantages," says E.J. Lee, corporate systems manager of Philip Morris Incorporated, "is that executives have to stand back and take a look at what they are trying to do in their function. You have to analyze the management of a function before you can put it on the machine."

SELECTION CRITERIA

About whom should information be included in an employee information system, and what information concerning each person should be collected? Since most firms find that they cannot do everything at once, they usually start with one specific group of people. The selection may be made on the basis of (1) salary class, (2) functional units or organizational groups, or (3) level of organization or corporate units.

Salary grades or exempt status may provide one type of classification for the particular files or systems. Companies need various kinds of information about people, depending on whether employees are salaried, hourly, exempt or nonexempt (from the Fair Labor Standards Act). Salary data on top executives or foreign service personnel may be kept in separate files or systems to insure security or to deal with special problems in processing. Different reports are required, and different information may be necessary for nonexempt peo-

EXHIBIT 7. *Amount of Data Required at Various Organizational Levels*

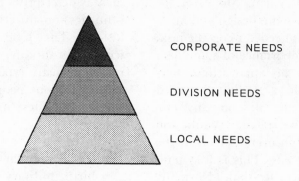

Source: Arthur Cassell
International Business Machines Corporation

ple than for exempt employees. In some companies salary status and exempt status are synonymous; in others they are not. Sometimes union and nonunion status are sufficiently different to warrant separate files and information.

In some companies personnel executives decided that initially they would include only certain functional units or specific organizational groups. In one case the personnel department was the first unit to be included in the files; it was selected to be part of a "shakedown cruise." In other companies a sales division or an engineering group was chosen. These organizational units sometimes have separate personnel arrangements and, therefore, are logically the first to be included in files such as skills inventory. In several companies that the author visited, skills inventories are limited to engineering or scientific personnel and possibly a few other "special skills" personnel.

Decentralized organizations frequently make a distinction between the amount and kind of employee information that is reported to the corporate level and that is required for divisional or local operations. IBM believes that a broad base of information is necessary to local operations, a more restricted amount should be reported to divisional offices, and a somewhat lesser number of data elements need to be reported to corporate headquarters. (See Exhibit 7.) Honeywell developed standard data-element definitions and configurations for approximately 537 data elements that might be used in its divisions, but fewer than 30 of these are reported to the corporate office for use in generating corporate reports.

It is characteristic of the firms studied that, because of geography, corporate structure, or decentralized management, plants in remote locations or loosely federated subsidiaries are not immediately included in the initial design and implementation of employee information systems. Since technical and organizational problems inherent in implementing systems are large, most firms make their initial attempts under the most favorable circumstances they can arrange and then try to avoid all unnecessary complications.

WHAT SHOULD BE IN A DATA BASE?

As mentioned previously, many companies report that they started out with hopes and expectations that were scaled down somewhat as they proceeded into the task of implementing a system. Moreover, as companies get into systems design and more closely define what is needed to do the task, they find that the importance of some data and the priorities of applications may change. For example, regarding the need for information about all company employees, one executive stated, "Would you keep the same data on every person in the company? Probably not. This is a systems design and analysis decision. Normally you would keep more data on some people than on others."

A manager in another company states, "At first we asked, 'If we want all people data, what should we collect?' Then we cut this down." In one eastern manufacturing company an executive says, "Originally we were going to include everything, but then we decided against starting a skills inventory. We already have a separate card system for recruiting. What we did include were descriptive data on a person, current job status and work history, plus coded data about performance appraisal, education and training, language abilities, benefits, and time-card and payroll data." In another firm an executive remarks, "When we asked, 'What would we like to know about people?' the list got too long. So at the corporate level we started with a finite list of data elements that were justified as necessary by users of the information and derived from previous reports to our corporate offices. We don't add to the list unless there is a valid reason for doing so."

These comments describe only a few ways in which companies scale down employee information by grappling with the realities of the situation.

Generally, the major categories of personnel information are (1) employee-related data, (2) job-related data, and (3) recruitment or procurement data. More specifically, personnel information is usually divided into a number of subcategories, such as descriptive personal data, skills inventories, organizational status, and work history. The following classification describes the subcategories in detail to illustrate the many types of data that may be recorded about people, without specifying the various files in which they might be placed:

- Descriptive data: name, address, date of birth, military status, and other data that describe a person.
- Skills inventory: a specialized application of descriptive data, such as skills, abilities, job experience, and interests. These data may refer to periods both before and after the employee is hired.
- Organizational status: date of hire, organization location, job title, and other job-related data indicating where a person is situated and what work he is doing in the organization.
- Work history: a compilation of past organizational positions, performance, and status changes—including raises and changes in location and budget center. This information may be accumulated from the date of hire, but usually it includes only the most recent 15 to 20 lines of data, covering approximately two to five years of activity.
- Performance appraisal: usually considered highly sensitive data; therefore, appraisal information and promotion potential are often coded.
- Wage and salary: all information necessary for wage and salary and benefits administration, as well as that necessary for calculation of gross payroll and gross-to-net pay.
- Labor reporting data: timekeeping, absence, production, and labor cost information; work location; supervisor to whom charged; and so forth.

EXHIBIT 8. *Employee Information Systems (Ford Motor Company)*

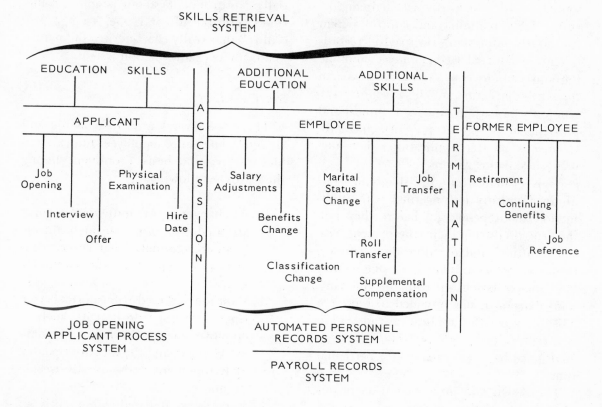

Used with the permission of the Ford Motor Company

- Vacation scheduling and control, health and safety, education and training information, as well as grievances, company transportation, and other data needed to support special programs.
- Recruitment: applications in process, applications on file, status of recruiting activity, data about schools, and follow-up information.
- Special data banks for research, such as attitude surveys; manpower development, organization planning, and selection studies; and manpower market analyses.
- Some firms are also developing non-computerized data banks containing information about the external envi-

ronment that relates to manpower acquisition and planning.

Since these subcategories are often detailed further, listings of data elements from files studied in several companies are shown in Appendix *A*.

Ford Motor Company's employee information systems, shown in Exhibit 8, illustrate that the various types of personnel data serve as elements in several systems and thus can mesh or interrelate these systems. Not all data relating to each of these activities need to be computer-processed; some can be manipulated by hand, while other data can be processed on electronic accounting machines (EAM) with card systems. This diagram indicates that there are several interrelated systems: an automated personnel records system (for salaried employees), a labor planning and control system (for hourly employees), two payroll records systems (one for salaried employees and one for hourly employees), a recruitment system (presently on cards), a skills-inventory system (only for certain kinds of technical and professional people at present), and miscellaneous smaller applications that augment these major systems.

As is evident from the diagram, Ford Motor Company is concerned with information about people (a) before they join the firm, (b) during their employment with the company, and (c) after their employment has been terminated, as long as they have some relationship with the company. This diagram is not intended to represent a list of all possible applications; instead, it is a representation of interrelated systems envisioned by one company at a particular time.

The design and implementation of employee information systems will be discussed in Chapter 3, in addition to the identification of items that have taken precedence over others—and the reasons for their selection—in the various companies studied.

Data Collection, Auditing, Manipulation, and Filing

Only three basic transactions can be made in a personnel file: (1) A record can be added to it, (2) a record can be changed, and (3) a record can be deleted. Once a company determines who should be included in the file and what information should be kept on each person, it has to establish how to change records so that they will reflect current activities and how to delete obsolete records and information

from the files. Although the process of initially capturing data about people is sometimes very difficult, it is the "change procedure" that really characterizes the nature of an employee information system.

SYSTEM INPUTS

There are several ways to schedule and channel data into employee information files on a regular basis. Prominent among these are the following:

1. As changes occur, individual records are updated, often through on-site "remote terminals" that enter information directly into the computer file.
2. Data are gathered from normal, routinely processed documents, such as employee-change notices; the data are batched, and the files are updated at frequent intervals—usually weekly or monthly.
3. Records are updated infrequently on a periodic basis, following a "one shot" collection of data on all members of the organization whose records are on file—for example, data are collected annually to update a skills-inventory file. Variations of this method are (a) mass updating, which results from widespread changes such as an across-the-board wage increase, and (b) cycle billing, in which perhaps one-twelfth of the employees would have their records updated each month—which is the practice of some companies in administering their performance appraisal systems.

Several of the companies studied have decided that the best way to handle inputs is to establish a single, computer-produced document that serves two purposes: (1)

provides a record or profile on the employee, which is kept by his supervisor or the local personnel office and (2) is used as an input document for recording changes in status or descriptive information about the employee. All changes or deletions are input to the system by means of the machine-produced document, which also serves as a record showing what the employee "looks like" to the company, as reflected by the central files. (See Exhibit 9.)

After pulling a copy of the machine-generated form from the local files, the supervisor or local personnel manager notes the appropriate changes on the form. It then is routed through normal channels, edited by the next higher personnel office, and is sent to keypunch. Later it is entered into regular file update and maintenance. During the first part of file update, the change may be audited manually or by machine for compliance with company and personnel policy, before it enters the machine-processing cycle. Afterward, a copy of the employee's new record is sent to the local office for comparison with the old record to insure that the change was made as requested by the originator.

This system is advantageous because it accomplishes a number of necessary activities. Management and personnel people can see what an employee "looks like" to the company by simply searching the files. If the information is made available to the employee, as in the case of skills inventory, he, too, can see how he looks to the company. Also, local management has a means of checking to insure that changes were made correctly. And, if information is to be used in files other than the primary one, transactions against one file can be batched on tape or cards and processed against another file when it is next updated. For example, if payroll data are stored in a separate system, relevant changes in personnel data

may be input to payroll files by tape or cards, without the necessity of processing any other documents manually. The "signature copy," showing approvals, may be sent to the appropriate personnel office for storage and reference.

At IBM, according to personnel services manager Arthur Cassell, "Every manager has a profile on his employees, and he also has responsibility for updating. It is his source document for performance appraisal, merit increases, and other changes in status." The input and processing procedures followed by IBM in making changes on employee records are shown in Exhibit 10.

Not all companies interviewed have this type of input routine. Some companies report that part of their personnel data is input by periodically sending out questionnaires to collect descriptive data. These are batched and all records are updated at one time. In some cases the cycle-billing method is used, with a portion of the forms being processed each month. In other cases, companies still use forms that are manually produced—instead of newer ones that are machine-produced—to collect data and keypunch inputs. Some companies use a special set of forms designed specifically for ease of keypunching and comparison of the new employee record with the old record. Generally, companies report that the most superior method is one that ties input to the computer with a computer-produced document and provides routine reporting on a regular basis.

As previously indicated, a number of companies have developed the ability to make mass changes of certain data elements in their files. This capability is particularly useful in companies that follow the practice of giving across-the-board wage increases, since they need to change all their file records simultaneously.

EXHIBIT 9. *Employee Record and Change Notice*

EMPLOYEE RECORD AND CHANGE NOTICE

1. DO NOT ENTER DATA IN SHADED DATA BOXES.
2. APPROPRIATE CODE REFERENCES APPEAR ON REVERSE SIDE.

EXHIBIT 9 (*continued*)

CODE INDEX

COMPLETE INSTRUCTIONS WITH CODE DEFINITIONS APPEAR IN PERSONNEL POLICY MANUAL. SEE POLICIES 201.1 (FIELD), 202 (_____ SALARIED), OR 203 (_____ HOURLY) FOR INFORMATION AS NEEDED.

CARD 310-TITLE CODES
1 - MR.
2 - DR. (MALE)
6 - MISS
7 - MRS.
8 - DR. (FEMALE)

CARD 310-MARITAL CODES
1 - SINGLE
2 - MARRIED
3 - SEPARATED OR DIVORCED
4 - WIDOWED
5 - SINGLE AND HEAD OF HOUSEHOLD

CARD 314-PERFORMANCE APPRAISAL CODES
ONE OF THE ALPHABETIC CODES BELOW WILL BE USED TO IDENTIFY THE TYPE OF APPRAISAL IN ALL COMPENSATION PROGRAMS. ENTER THIS CODE AS THE PREFIX OR FIRST DIGIT OF THE REQUIRED TWO DIGIT CODE AS APPLICABLE.
A - THREE MONTH APPRAISAL
B - SIX MONTH APPRAISAL
C - TWELVE MONTH APPRAISAL
D - SPECIAL APPRAISAL
THE PERFORMANCE RATING WILL BE ENTERED AS THE SECOND DIGIT OF THE TWO DIGIT CODE. CHOOSE THE APPROPRIATE CODE BELOW ACCORDING TO THE EMPLOYEE'S RATING AND THE APPLICABLE COMPENSATION PROGRAM:
(EXEMPT NON-SELLING-COMP. PROGRAMS)
1 - A
2 - B
3 - C
4 - D
5 - E
6 - F
7 - G
(EXEMPT SELLING AND TECH. REP.-COMP. PROGRAMS)
1 - UNSATISFACTORY
2 - FAIR
3 - GOOD
4 - VERY GOOD
5 - EXCEPTIONAL
(NON-EXEMPT _____ AND FIELD WKLY.-COMP. PROGRAMS)
1 - UNSATISFACTORY
2 - FAIR
3 - LOW GOOD
4 - HIGH GOOD
5 - VERY GOOD
6 - EXCEPTIONAL

CARD 321-SENIORITY UNIT CODES
A - OPERATING ENGINEERS
M - MACHINE MANUFACTURING
C - CLEANING
S - SERVICE AND SUPPLY
X - _____ SUPPLY
P - PHOTO

CARD 315-RATE CHANGE CODES
SALARY INCREASES (SALARIED EMPLOYEES)
50 - MERIT INCREASE-THREE MONTH (TECH REPS ONLY)
51 - MERIT INCREASE-SEMI-ANNUAL
52 - MERIT INCREASE-ANNUAL
53 - SPECIAL MERIT INCREASE
54 - COMBINED MERIT AND PROMOTIONAL INCREASE
61 - ONE GRADE PROMOTIONAL INCREASE
62 - TWO GRADE PROMOTIONAL INCREASE
63 - THREE OR MORE GRADE PROMOTIONAL INCREASE
64 - PROMOTIONAL INCREASE FROM NON-EXEMPT (HOURLY OR WEEKLY) TO EXEMPT
65 - PROMOTIONAL INCREASE FROM NON-EXEMPT (HOURLY) TO NON-EXEMPT (WEEKLY)
60 - PROMOTIONAL INCREASE
81 - ADJUSTMENT TO MINIMUM INCREASE
82 - RELATIONSHIP ADJUSTMENT INCREASE
83 - RELOCATION ADJUSTMENT INCREASE
85 - COMBINED ADJUSTMENT TO MINIMUM AND MERIT INCREASE
86 - COMBINED ADJUSTMENT TO MINIMUM AND PROMOTIONAL INCREASE
SALARY DECREASES (SALARIED EMPLOYEES)
70 - DEMOTIONAL INCREASE
71 - DEMOTIONAL DECREASE FROM EXEMPT TO NON-EXEMPT
84 - RELOCATION ADJUSTMENT DECREASE
OTHER SALARY CHANGES
59 - NEW HIRE RATE (DO NOT USE-FOR INFORMATION ONLY)
89 - SALARY ADJUSTMENT
RATE CHANGES (HOURLY ONLY)
90 - GENERAL INCREASE
91 - PROGRESSION INCREASE
92 - 100% EFFICIENCY THREE CONSECUTIVE MONTHS INCREASE
93 - SPECIAL UNION AGREEMENT RATE ADJUSTMENT
94 - INEQUITY ADJUSTMENT
95 - RE-EVALUATION ADJUSTMENT
96 - PROMOTIONAL INCREASE
97 - DOWNGRADING RATE ADJUSTMENT
98 - RATE ADJUSTMENT-LATERAL TRANSFER

CARD 333-MEDICAL INSURANCE CODES
(BASIC MEDICAL COVERAGE)
00 - NONE
11 - HOURLY, SINGLE
12 - HOURLY, DEPENDENT
13 - HOURLY, AGE 19 WAIVER
21 - _____, SALARIED, SINGLE
23 - _____, SALARIED, DEPENDENT
31 - FIELD, SINGLE
32 - FIELD, DEPENDENT
33 - FIELD, AGE 19 WAIVER
(MAJOR MEDICAL COVERAGE)
0 - NONE
1 - HOURLY, SINGLE
2 - WEEKLY, SINGLE
3 - CANADIAN, SINGLE
4 - WEEKLY, DEPENDENT
5 - WEEKLY, DEPENDENT
6 - CANADIAN DEPENDENT
7 - OTHER EMPLOYEES, SINGLE
8 - OTHER EMPLOYEES, DEPENDENT

CARD 320-JOB CHANGE CODES
PROMOTIONS
11 - ONE GRADE PROMOTION
12 - TWO GRADE PROMOTION
13 - THREE OR MORE GRADE PROMOTION
14 - PROMOTION FROM NON-EXEMPT (HOURLY OR WEEKLY) TO EXEMPT
15 - PROMOTION FROM NON-EXEMPT (HOURLY) TO NON-EXEMPT (WEEKLY)
10 - ALL OTHER PROMOTIONS (SALARIED ONLY)
16 - PROMOTION (HOURLY ONLY)
44 - RE-EVALUATION TO A HIGHER GRADE
DEMOTIONS OR DOWNGRADES
20 - DEMOTION
21 - DEMOTION FROM EXEMPT TO NON-EXEMPT
23 - DOWNGRADE (HOURLY ONLY)
32 - TRANSFER TO POSITION IN LOWER GRADE (MAINTAINED SALARY LEVEL)
46 - RE-EVALUATION TO A LOWER GRADE
TRANSFERS-NOT INVOLVING PROMOTION OR DEMOTION
30 - LATERAL TRANSFER TO NEW ORGANIZATION IN SAME JOB
31 - LATERAL TRANSFER TO NEW ORGANIZATION AND DIFFERENT JOB
36 - LATERAL TRANSFER IN SAME ORGANIZATION TO DIFFERENT JOB
33 - ASSIGNMENT ON/OR RETURN FROM TEMPORARY ASSIGNMENT
ADMINISTRATIVE CHANGES-DO NOT ENTER THESE CODES-FOR INFORMATION ONLY
40 - CHANGE OF JOB TITLE
41 - ADMINISTRATIVE JOB CODE CHANGE
45 - ADMINISTRATIVE ORGANIZATION CODE CHANGE
49 - NEW HIRE JOB ASSIGNMENT

CARD 332-EMPLOYMENT STATUS CODES
(REGULAR FULL TIME)
01 - NEW HIRE
02 - REINSTATED (AFTER ABSENCE)
03 - FORMER CO-OP
04 - FORMER TEMP. FULL TIME
05 - FORMER REG. PART-TIME
06 - FORMER TEMP. PART-TIME
(TEMP. FULL-TIME)
21 - NEW HIRE
22 - REINSTATED
23 - FORMER CO-OP
(REG. PART-TIME)
41 - NEW HIRE
42 - REINSTATED
43 - FORMER CO-OP
(TEMP. PART-TIME)
61 - NEW HIRE
62 - REINSTATED
63 - FORMER CO-OP
(CO-OP PART-TIME)
81 - NEW HIRE
(CO-OP WORK BLOCK)
91 - NEW HIRE
92 - REINSTATED

CARD 327-INACTIVE STATUS CODES
(RESIGNATIONS)
10 - RESIGNATION WHILE ON LAYOFF
11 - ACCEPT OTHER EMPLOYMENT
12 - JOB DISSATISFACTION
13 - MOVING TO NEW LOCATION
14 - PURSUANCE OF DOMESTIC DUTIES OR PREGNANCY
15 - ATTEND SCHOOL FULL TIME (EXCLUDES SUMMER EMPLOYEES AND CO-OPS-SEE CODES 40 AND 69)
16 - FAILURE TO REPORT FOR WORK
17 - PERSONAL REASONS
18 - POOR HEALTH
19 - MUTUALLY SATISFACTORY RELEASE
(INVOLUNTARY TERMINATIONS)
20 - EXPIRED LAYOFF RIGHTS
21 - FLAGRANT DISREGARD OF COMPANY INTEREST
22 - DISHONESTY
23 - INSUBORDINATION
24 - CHRONIC ABSENTEEISM OR TARDINESS
25 - PERSONALITY CONFLICT
26 - DUAL SERVITUDE
27 - INAPTITUDE FOR JOB
28 - RELEASE
29 - PHYSICAL OR MENTAL IMPAIRMENT
(OTHER)
40 - END OF TEMPORARY WORK
45 - DEATH
50 - LAYOFF
60 - TRANSFER TO SUBSIDIARY
69 - CO-OP RETURN TO SCHOOL
80 - RETIREMENT
(LEAVES OF ABSENCE)
70 - MILITARY LEAVE
71 - PERSONAL LEAVE
72 - MATERNITY LEAVE-UNCONDITIONAL
73 - MATERNITY LEAVE-CONDITIONAL
74 - EDUCATIONAL LEAVE

CARD 323-PAY METHOD NUMBERS
0 - WEEKLY, CANADIAN
1 - HOURLY
2 - WEEKLY,
3 - EXEMPT,
4 - EXEMPT, CANADIAN
5 - EXEMPT, FIELD
6 - CONFIDENTIAL
7 - WEEKLY TECHNICAL REPRESENTATIVES
8 - FAST PAY (ASSIGNED BY PAYROLL ONLY)
9 - ALL BRANCH, ZONE, _____ AND _____ CLERICAL AND PRODUCTION PERSONNEL

CARD 316-MAINT. OR SPEC. RATES (HOURLY)
A - ONE MONTH MAINTAINED RATE
B - RIT MAINTAINED RATE
C - RED CIRCLE MAINTAINED RATE-JOB ELIMINATION
D - RED CIRCLE MAINTAINED RATE-JOB EVALUATION
E - SHOP CHAIRMAN SPECIAL RATE
F - SUPPLEMENTAL COMPENSATION RATE
G - OTHER SPECIAL OR MAINTAINED RATE
R - REMOVAL OF MAINTAINED OR SPECIAL RATE

EXHIBIT 10. *Input to and Processing of an Employee-Change Notice and Record*

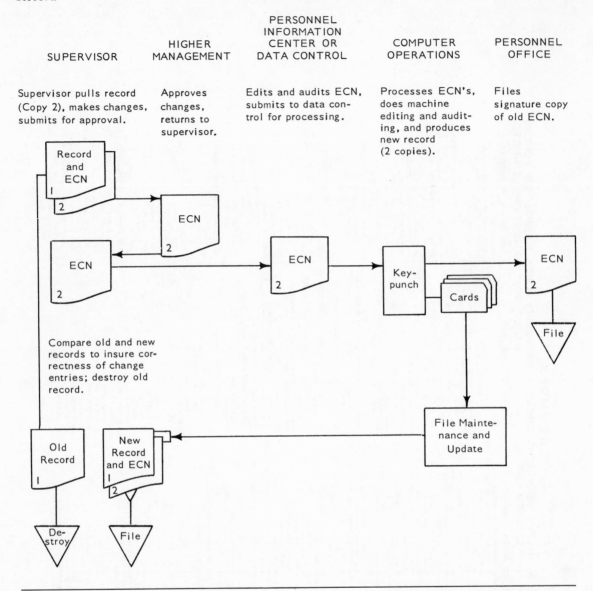

SUPERVISOR	HIGHER MANAGEMENT	PERSONNEL INFORMATION CENTER OR DATA CONTROL	COMPUTER OPERATIONS	PERSONNEL OFFICE
Supervisor pulls record (Copy 2), makes changes, submits for approval.	Approves changes, returns to supervisor.	Edits and audits ECN, submits to data control for processing.	Processes ECN's, does machine editing and auditing, and produces new record (2 copies).	Files signature copy of old ECN.

Compare old and new records to insure correctness of change entries; destroy old record.

In summary, inputs may be made to files in the following ways:

- On a one-shot basis, for data on one or more persons.
- With a manually processed document in the course of regular data processing.
- Use of a record/report type of document, on which changes can be entered and which is initiated by the computer, processed through the cycle, and returned for use as a record.
- Mass changes, usually initiated by the personnel office.
- A fifth method is direct access through remote terminals, by which information is either entered directly into the

record or kept on a batching tape until the next file update, which may be at the time of the regular file maintenance or when reports on the data are requested.

EDITING AND AUDITING DATA INPUTS

One executive reports that, when employees are moved from one position to another and documents are prepared to process the change, 80 to 85 percent of the information on the documents does not change. Since the company does not have record/report forms generated by machine, it was using Flexowriters to reproduce the unchanged portions of the records. It had found that numerous errors are made when changes are prepared manually; in fact, 30 percent of the change forms had one or more errors. These errors are detected by eye; then, either they are corrected on the spot, or the document is returned to the originator for correction or redrawing. Ten percent of the documents have to be redone completely.

Errors are not, as the company assumed at first, clerical in nature. Over half are "logical" errors—that is, they fail to meet policy requirements. Therefore, management decided to build checks into a validation or audit routine, which would permit the data to be checked without fail every time they were processed by the computer.

This example confirms the computer's ability to provide the critical function of insuring the accuracy of data and the validity of actions taken throughout an organization.

As used in this report, *editing* means visually or mechanically checking to insure that data elements have the proper configuration—letters in fields or spaces that require letters, numbers in appropriate fields or spaces, elements of the proper length, and so on. *Auditing* refers to checking the validity of data against predetermined standards, such as confirming that at least ten months have elapsed since an employee's last raise, if the company has a policy to that effect.

The decision to edit and audit extensively by computer, rather than manually, is a critical one in an employee information system. By designing the system to take advantage of the unfailing rigor of machine logic and processing, companies can greatly reduce the problem of "garbage in–garbage out." Machine errors are almost nil. Machine logic does not vary; it is consistent and precise in each and every instance. Moreover, the computer has the capacity to check actions against policies and to insure consistency, thereby permitting management to check each action that occurs in the company, to the limit of specification that management wishes to prescribe. Although programming extensive auditing of transactions is expensive, the degree to which it is done determines the power of the computer to administer the company's personnel program on a routine basis.

DEVELOPING TRUST IN A DATA BASE

Developing an extensive machine audit program raises some complex questions about how to handle invalid or inconsistent data when they are submitted for inclusion in the files. The problem hinges on what should be done with a document containing both valid and invalid data when it is received for processing. There are two characteristic solutions to this problem. One solution is to send the document back to the originator for correction before any data are entered into the file. Under this plan the originator is informed of his mistake; not only does he correct it, but he is also motivated to get it right the next time (if he wants it to go through on schedule). Further, the files will not contain any incorrect data that would show up in reports produced during the period between entry and correction.

The second solution to this problem is to accept documents containing both valid and invalid data, enter the data into the file, print out an "error message," and require the originator to clean up the errors. This method is used by the majority of companies studied during this survey.

The major drawback of the first solution is that, in the beginning, many erroneous inputs will be received; many actions, such as granting pay raises or recording transfers, will be delayed; and in general too much pressure is put on the line people to achieve perfection when it is not necessary. The second solution is based on the assumption that most of the data are right and that the rest can easily be cleaned up within a relatively short time. Moreover, the paychecks and reports will reflect the status of the organization with a reasonable degree of accuracy, even while the file is being cleaned up.

The desirability of each of these solutions depends upon the use of the system —is it primarily for reporting, or is it primarily for producing documents such as paychecks? If the system is used for reports, accuracy of data is probably more important. If it is used primarily to produce documents, then speed and immediacy are most important. Another factor that may influence selection is the relationship between files, which is discussed in a later section of this chapter.

Xerox Corporation accepts only valid information; when inconsistent or incorrect data are found on input documents, they are returned for correction. One manager says, "This makes a lot of managers mad, but the people in Finance know that our files are 99.5 percent correct and that they can count on the files for accurate information when they need it."

At IBM the second method is followed. When the company installed the system, its first attempts to process the files resulted in over 5,000 pages of audit messages. In an effort to clean up the system, one of the divisions set up a system of rating its personnel managers on the accuracy of their inputs to the corporate file. These efforts have now reduced the identifiable errors to a statistically tolerable amount.

All firms have the problem of achieving and maintaining accuracy of data in computer files and of developing faith in these files. Philip Morgan, of Information Science, states that accuracy may be achieved by taking the following steps:

1. Use a mechanical method of retaining backup files—grandfather, father, and son (present) files—so that destroying a file during processing does not result in having to regenerate it from scratch.

2. Insure that what was intended to go into the files actually got there. Audit programs, validate data, and check them on a "likelihood" and consistency basis; then reject data if errors are found in a "critical" element, such as file number, Social Security number, or amount of pay increase.

3. In editing programs, insure that information—or a tape—is received from every department or division that should submit data; get agreement from these groups to provide the data; and set up a method of correcting any errors discovered during processing.

4. Send a newly updated file impression back to the originator, to be checked to insure that the data reflect current changes.

5. Create a listing of the types of transactions processed during file updating. This listing shows an audit trail,

which should be checked by both users and systems people to insure consistency with systems parameters and details, as well as with local conditions.

6. Maintain accuracy at the local level by spot checking data in files with users at each location.

Maintaining data accuracy in this manner requires a mixture, and coordination, of hardware, organization, structure, and human factors. All are important, but establishing responsibility is sometimes difficult. Although the user has primary responsibility for the data he provides, the systems people also have a dominant role. In addition, the personnel department occupies a key spot. Therefore, data accuracy can be achieved only when responsibility is shared.

Reporting Information
out of a System

The basic purpose of an information system is to collect, store, and process information so that it can be reported out when it is wanted and needed. To be effective, an employee information system must have a capacity powerful enough to report timely data in a highly usable form.

When an employee information system does not have a capacity adequate to report out data when needed, or in the format that is most usable by managers, frustration results. Saul Citrone, manager, medical personnel data systems at IBM, states, "You can have the most detailed data bank in the world, but if you can't get the information out of it, it is useless." This problem is a constant source of frustration to managers and a source of conflict between users and systems people. The typical management

complaint is, "Why can't I get the information that I want, when I want it, out of that system?" The typical response from systems people is, "You didn't thoroughly think through what you wanted beforehand. Now you are asking for something that the system wasn't designed to produce."

Successful employee information systems resolve this problem by providing three features: the ability to access any data elements in a file, the capacity to operate on these data in many ways, and the flexibility to report out information in a variety of formats. With such features, managers need not anticipate all the questions they may ask sometime in the future. However, developing such flexibility and capacity costs money.

Types of Reports

During this study the author saw a tremendous number of employee information reports of various types and formats. The reports were designed to meet the needs of personnel departments, executives, agencies outside the company, individual employees, and others. No widely used formats or designs were found. As might be expected, all the reports were designed to meet the specific needs and customary methods used by each company in doing business. However, such reports can be classified according to two major criteria: (1) when and why they are produced and (2) design and medium, which are determined by their use. (See Exhibit 11.)

When and why reports are produced. Reports may be classified according to whether they contain routine, special, or demand information. *Routine reports* are produced at regular intervals, usually during the regular file-maintenance cycle. At this time, when the files are being updated to reflect the current status of company operations, reports that show the latest in-

EXHIBIT 11. *Classification of Reports from an Employee Information System*

WHEN PRODUCED	DESIGN AND MEDIUM
Routine Reports	Listings
(Produced during file maintenance and update.)	Preprinted Records
	Microfilm
Special Reports	Notifications
(Produced on request.)	Exception Reports
Demand Information	Answers to Single Questions
(Produced by real-time access and often shown on a cathode-ray tube.)	(Format specified by questioner.)
	Optical Scanning

formation are often generated. Many file-maintenance programs require examination of every record in the file. Therefore, voluminous reports are more economical to produce during the maintenance cycle than at other times. Executives frequently want to see specific data from the most recent file transactions. Through the use of control cards, regular reports, such as quarterly reports, may be generated or even suppressed if desired.

Special reports are produced on request or on an "as needed" basis. They are usually designed to answer one-shot, nonrecurring questions and are often in a format appropriate to the question. Special programs may be written and processed against a file on a request basis to access information for this type of question. Often, the same report program may be slightly tailored, or patched, to select different information, sort data differently, or present data in a slightly different format. The major problem in using this approach to generate special reports is that each search for information requires programming effort. Since programming effort is sparse in most companies, even a very simple report may be delayed a long time before it is available to the user.

This problem may be alleviated by report-generator programs that are more general and can access any element of data from a single data file, or perhaps from several similar files. Such programs have the capability to operate on data in many ways —sorting, accumulating totals, and performing mathematical or algebraic calculations —and they have the flexibility to produce reports in various formats. Although the initial cost of these programs is considerably greater than single-purpose report generators, their flexibility and capacity make them extremely valuable tools in an employee information system.

Demand information reports are even more sophisticated. An executive may formulate questions, call the appropriate file of the computer, interrogate it, and almost instantly receive answers on an optical scanning device—all without leaving his desk. Although this type of report may seem futuristic to some executives, it is not very far in the future. Richard Bueschel, president of Time Share Corporation, states that capabilities to request and receive "instant information" will exist in many personnel offices by the early 1970's. Thus technological developments may result in new types of personnel executives—men who can make productive use of computer equipment and technology.

A variation of this demand information is being used by the personnel departments of several companies interviewed for this study. Mobil Oil, Ford, IBM, McDonnell Douglas, and others use remote terminals, situated away from the computer area.

Since some of these applications are discussed later in the report, one example will illustrate the point. At Mobil Oil Company, searches of skills inventory are made by a personnel executive—a nonprogrammer—who writes simple instructions for the search and criteria for the selection of candidates and specifies the print format of the information he wishes to have printed out for each person selected. These instructions are entered into the computer through a remote terminal, and within a minute or less he receives a typed message giving him the requested information on those candidates selected from the file. This real-time system is used by several functions of numerous companies, so it will probably be used extensively by personnel departments within a relatively short time.

Design and medium of report. Reports may also be classified according to format or form. The most common type of report is a *listing* of items in a file, called a tab run. Using a specified format, tab runs list data elements from each record selected from a file. The advantage of such a listing is that it may be scanned by eye to spot variations in data elements that are common to many records. The greatest weakness of a tab run is that it does require visual inspection. Such inspection may be conducted much more quickly and accurately by machine.

Another type of report is *statistical* in its presentation. It may be prepared by the computer and show counts, arrays, statistical means, standard deviations, and percentages, which may be presented in the form of graphs, charts, and so forth. This kind of report is prevalent in wage and salary applications and in benefits analyses of companies such as Ford, IBM, and Standard Oil (Ohio).

As was discussed earlier, several companies are using the computer to produce *preprinted* employee profiles—forms on which data from the files are printed before they leave the computer area. The computer is also used to produce *notifications* of activities that are to take place according to a prearranged schedule, such as notifications that performance appraisals for particular employees are due. In IBM and a few other companies, the computer is used to chart the organization. Several firms are developing an application of an organization tree for use in wage and salary administration and for organization planning.

The *exception report* is especially valuable to companies. This report is limited to those data that fall outside predetermined parameters—that is, unless an item is an exception to the rule, it does not appear on the report. The range of possible uses for this kind of reporting has not been well developed by most companies at this time, but it has tremendous potential. For example, a company might use exception reports to spot policy violations in a myriad of places, locate the sources, and then find out why the violations occurred.

One-shot questions and optical scanning devices have already been discussed, and nothing more will be said about them here except to note that the format and style of these reports are limited only by the imagination of the user.

A final report medium is *microfilm*. Data can be transferred directly from tape to microfilm with a Stromberg-Carlson machine. At Eastman Kodak these microfilm strips are used for such purposes as locator files and storage of narrative data about employees. The added capacity to search coded data on microfilm enables companies to store and retrieve narrative data about performance appraisal, recruitment evaluation, and other similar kinds of data.

Problems in Designing Reports

Two basic problems face personnel, systems, and line management in their efforts to design effective employee information reporting systems: (1) What information does management need? and (2) How should programs be designed to provide timely, easily accessible information in a form readily usable by management and others in an organization? It is difficult for managers to define and communicate their information needs. They cannot always determine what information they will want or need, or the form in which it should be reported. Greater sophistication and more experience are needed to improve these communication blocks, especially in companies that must respond quickly to changes in their environments. Change intensifies these problems in all organizations, regardless of size or industry.

Saul Citrone, of IBM, says, "Information systems in personnel are not responsive enough to the changing environment of personnel. We are no longer isolated; we have to live by rules set by others—both inside and outside our organization. Therefore, our systems must have very flexible capabilities."

In general, both systems and personnel people who were interviewed agree that systems must be designed with very flexible reporting capabilities. These capabilities should provide at least four features: (1) timeliness, (2) the ability to select any desired element of data from each record in the file, (3) the capacity to operate extensively on numerical data, and (4) the capability to report information in any desired format.

Interrelationships of Files

As mentioned previously, when companies begin to develop an employee information system, they sometimes want to include all information about employees in one data base. At first glance this seems to be a logical approach, but in practice it has not worked out well. There are a number of very practical reasons why firms have developed multiple-file employee information systems.

First, establishing a single data base containing all information about everybody in the company is a very large, complicated task. An incremental approach is easier and more practical.

Second, different kinds of information are applicable to different tasks and serve different purposes. Philip Morgan, of Information Science, illustrates this with his comment: "The purpose of a payroll file is for paying and the purpose of a personnel file is for personnel. In general, these files must be linked, but not necessarily in the same data base."

The third reason for establishing separate files is cost. Processing a large data file is very expensive. A small, single-purpose file has fewer potential applications, but it also costs less to process.

Fourth, capturing and processing various kinds of data require different types of reporting and different processing cycles. For example, rate and position changes may be captured from regularly processed employee-change notices, while skills inventory data are collected and updated on special forms, usually on an annual basis. One kind of form is processed on a more or less regular basis, while the other is normally a one-shot, batch process.

Fifth, some information changes rather often, while other information is comparatively static. In skills inventory, for example, location changes are relatively common, but skills additions or deletions generally show very little change, except over long periods of time.

A sixth reason for establishing separate files is a need for security for certain kinds of information. In some companies, performance appraisal data are considered to be the most sensitive information maintained in employee records. In other companies, top management payrolls are separated from other payroll information because they are considered sensitive.

A seventh reason is rivalry among groups, departments, and divisions. Although interdepartmental politics may not seem a logical reason for establishing separate employee information files, it is a fact of life in some firms. For example, some finance departments refuse to tie the payroll system to a personnel information system simply because they do not trust the personnel department to provide accurate, timely data for inclusion in the payroll files.

The final reason for the separation of files is that some information is not systematized or defined well enough to be included when the files are being designed. Often, companies have deferred including skills-inventory information because, as one personnel executive explained, "The managers don't know exactly what they want to go into the file."

TYPES OF FILES

It is evident that there is little, or no, uniformity among companies in their selection, development, and use of employee information files. Yet certain basic data are needed by all companies. The firms interviewed for this study use the following types of files:

- Payroll (salary, hourly, and special executive).
- Benefits (for example, deferred compensation and stock options).
- Personnel descriptive data and work history.
- Training and education.
- Performance appraisal.
- Foreign service and foreign language competence.

- Skills inventory.
- Management development information.
- Labor reporting.
- Timekeeping.
- Absences.
- Manpower planning.
- Vacation scheduling.
- Medical data.
- Transportation.
- Attitude survey information.
- Accession/separation.

One or more of the interviewed companies have disk, tape, or card files bearing the titles listed above. Most of these data files are combined, in each case by one or more of the companies that participated in the survey, but the combinations vary. For example, in some firms salary payroll files include all salaried employees, up to and including the president. In other companies the executive payroll file is separate. Some personnel data files contain only descriptive data, while others include work history, training and education information, performance appraisal data, and langauge abilities. Some management development files contain education and performance appraisal data, plus limited skills-inventory information. Absence data of one company come from a timekeeping file, while in another they are kept in a separate file. The combinations are numerous.

FILE MAINTENANCE

The purpose of file maintenance is to update, or bring new information into a file, and to put it in its proper place in the file records so that it can be retrieved at some future time. During this updating cycle, companies often prepare reports that reflect the current status of information in the updated file. They find that they can achieve greater efficiencies if at this time they select out those data required for reports, sort the items, and perform computations on them—especially in tape files.

Keeping erroneous information out of the files is highly desirable. Because incorrect data-element configurations can cause the computer to reject data, incoming data are subjected to editing and auditing to insure validity and correct configurations. Inputs may come from routine documents processed elsewhere in the organization or directly from some other computerized data file. The power, or capability, of a program is greatly increased if it can interact mechanically with other data files and receive inputs from keypunched input documents. If a report-generator program can draw information from several computerized files of information, its capability is even greater. (Systems that can move information from one file to another, and draw information for reports from more than one file simultaneously, are referred to as "integrated," and the individual files within them are called "modules.")

RELATIONSHIPS AMONG FILES

There are many possible ways to relate various personnel data files. They may be separate and more or less unrelated, except that reports from each may be compared visually. They may be related in that they employ identical coding systems that permit some comparison of coded data, or at least permit selection of identical data elements from each file. Some files are related in that they can be cross-checked by the computer to insure commonality of records or specific data elements. A final relationship is that they may be integrated to permit updating of one file with data from another and the drawing of data from several files for incorporation in a single report.

Even if files are separate and unrelated, in the interest of developing a smooth, consistent system it is helpful to have inputs to the file flow from routinely processed documents, such as employee-change notices. Information captured in this manner is usually more reliable and accurate than that which is obtained by use of a special-purpose document, such as a questionnaire.

Common codes are helpful in the following way: When information from several files is to be compared or used in a common report, data elements referring to the same item must be defined in the same way and refer to precisely the same thing. Otherwise, people find themselves adding apples and oranges. File order is important if files are to be checked against one other to insure commonality of records. (One company reports that its request for information about an insurance program was sent to the home address of a former employee who had been deceased for several months. The mistake resulted from files that did not agree and thus could not be compared.)

Obviously, files are updated and outputs generated at different times. Many firms update their payroll files daily and produce employees' checks on a weekly or a biweekly basis, but they believe it necessary to update their personnel data files on only a monthly basis. If data from one file can be batched for input to another file at a later date, there is no need to keypunch the data twice, or to risk further human error that might cause disagreement between the information in the two files. Moreover, in some companies, IBM and Honeywell, for example, the first portion of each employee's local record—which is a specified number of digits of information—comprises the data required by corporate headquarters in generating corporate reports. This information is spun off during normal file maintenance, and the resulting tape is sent to corporate offices for their information and use.

Another variation of this technique results in a statistical file, an abbreviated version of critical information from the records of all employees in the file, which can be used to generate reports inexpensively between file-maintenance operations.

The Critical Relationship Between Payroll and Personnel Information

In all the companies interviewed, the relationship between payroll and personnel activities is pivotal. Since an obvious relationship exists between payroll and other personnel information, the logical question is: "Should payroll data and related personnel data be kept and processed in a single data base?" As might be expected, companies provide a variety of answers. In some firms the two files are only remotely related. In other companies they are closely interdependent. Some companies have difficulty in dealing with the interrelationship between payroll and personnel, while others experience no problems.

The question of what is the most favorable relationship between personnel and payroll information raises a number of issues. For example, in some companies interdepartmental rivalries and problems arising from conflicting values have to be resolved. Also, outputs of systems differ; and, if they are combined, tradeoffs must be worked out. There are problems related to approval loops and other input routines. Editing and auditing requirements are different and must be resolved. Timing, costs, and other processing demands must be considered. And, finally, the relationships between these two types of files and all

other employee information files in the company must be worked out. These considerations are not inconsequential.

Conflicts Between Departmental Values and Requirements

Of the 408 companies replying to the survey questionnaire, 89 percent report that they have computer-based payroll applications, and 67 percent report having personnel applications, in addition to their payroll applications. In all the firms interviewed, payroll applications preceded personnel applications—that is, historically, payroll was first. In several of the companies interviewed, computer operations and systems efforts are, or were, under the direction of the finance executive's or controller's function in the company organization. Of course, in most firms finance is responsible for payroll operations. In some companies, finance and payroll people openly admit that they have always had disdain for the way the personnel department handles data.

Relationships between personnel and payroll might be perceived as sizable hurdles when a personnel department wants to apply computers to its own data handling needs. In a few companies, personnel people groan about the difficulties they have encountered with payroll in developing computer programs; occasionally, they respond negatively. Some personnel people believe that finance is narrow and provincial in its viewpoint, that it lacks interest in the personnel department's problems, and that, in general, it is not very cooperative. Perhaps these statements are extreme; yet they characterize the situation in some companies. Their validity is not as important as their impact on the working relationships of people in the finance and personnel functions of a company.

There are real, as well as fancied, differences between the functional requirements of a payroll system and a personnel data system. However, the two are often interrelated inextricably. As reported earlier, Philip Morgan, of Information Science, notes that, although payroll and personnel files each support different activities and functions in a company, they need to be linked together, but they do not have to share the same data base.

But even linking them may cause problems, as the following comments disclose. When asked about this relationship, one payroll manager declared, "If I can pay people accurately and maintain corporate and government-required statistics, I have what I need to run payroll. And I couldn't care less if other invalid personnel information is in the system."

Another payroll man reports, "I don't need to know where a man is, or what he is doing. All I need is his pay rate."

A third payroll manager expressed the opinion that he doesn't need to know why a payroll action occurs; he is interested in only the amount and proper authorization.

Even if these attitudes are atypical, they show the limited perception of needs by one partner in the employee information system, and they indicate how he might react to any added restrictions that would frustrate his major concern of "getting out the payroll."

For the most part, employee information files are report-oriented rather than document-oriented. From personnel's point of view, management obviously needs many data elements other than just the rate of pay, type of rate change, and so on. If this information is to be of value, all the data going into the files have to be correct and consistent. If an input document has both valid and invalid data, then the incorrect data should be corrected as soon as possible,

or none of the data should be allowed to enter the data base. If inconsistent information exists in a data base, reports produced from it are subject to question by management and the integrity of the system may be jeopardized. On the other hand, if inputs to the system are rejected because data on the document are inconsistent, the transaction will be delayed—which runs counter to the values held by payroll people. But the time factor is often not so critical in a personnel system. Since neither alternative is a perfect solution, the best that can be achieved in practice is probably a workable compromise.

OTHER PROBLEM AREAS

The type of equipment often determines the feasibility of establishing a single data base. If random-access files are used, and programs permit operating on portions of the data file without disturbing the remainder, it is possible to avoid the expense of processing a total file to update only a small portion of it. Most of the firms studied, however, have tape systems that require processing the entire file of information during file maintenance. In such cases, the amount of data duplication between payroll and personnel records usually determines whether the files should be combined. Generally, the companies had separate files of information, more or less mechanically related to each other.

Most firms find it advantageous to provide the capability to update one file with data from another. If the files are set up so that the personnel file feeds the payroll file, then the personnel staff will find it relatively easy to get programming assistance, to keep their system in good repair, to make revisions required by organizational changes, and to audit their information. Moreover, it is likely that the personnel file will be updated more often and reports generated more frequently than would otherwise be the case.

The use of a common file-number order permits checking for commonality of records in various files. In some companies, the order of files is based on company-assigned employee numbers, while in others insurance numbers or Social Security numbers are used. Because the latter coding system seems to be the most serviceable, its use is gaining in popularity, even though foreign nationals must be assigned "dummy" numbers. Some companies have a variety of coding systems for various employee files, making it difficult to select or compare data elements that are often desirable to include in one report. Common codes may be expensive to achieve, but they are very useful.

A final problem that will be treated here is the inclusion of dissimilar data in the same file. Although there are advantages in having all the information in a single file so that it can be selected out for reports, there is one major disadvantage—whenever a portion of the data is processed in a tape system, the entire file must be "turned." If the file is large, that costs money. Many firms circumvent this problem by making their files compatible to the extent that reports can be generated from more than one file; they handle the maintenance and update of each file separately. In this way a payroll file can be updated daily, a personnel data file monthly, and both files coupled for the generation of a single report. Advances in equipment and hardware applications will very likely enable companies to develop more efficient personnel information systems in the future.

3. Designing and Implementing an Employee Information System

When a company begins the task of developing an employee information system, it is faced with a jumble of questions and possibilities. During the initial investigation, it soon becomes evident that the answer to one question depends on the answer to other questions and that each part seems to depend on other parts. These interrelated factors have to be sorted out and some basic decisions made before work can be started on some specific part of the overall project.

The company needs to establish the present state of its employee information handling, what it would like to do and why, what information is needed, and what methods to use for collecting, processing, and reporting that information. Strategies have to be mapped out, basic and immediate project objectives have to be set, and tactics and specific programs for developing the system have to be designed. All who will be affected by the information system need to be involved in the planning at this stage. And, of course, resources need to be obtained both to provide the facilities and the people and to perform the tasks required to establish the system.

The developmental process has three distinct phases: (1) predesign, (2) design, and (3) implementation. In the *predesign* phase, goals are set, feasibility studies are conducted, and priorities are established for the design and implementation of various portions of the system. Then strategies for gaining acceptance are mapped out, and plans are made for staffing and organizing a group to carry out the project. In the *de-sign phase,* company practices are examined to determine what is presently being done in handling employee information, and key decisions are made regarding the type of information needed by the company, the specific information required in the system, and how this information should be arranged in a data base. Input routines are defined, as are file-update and -maintenance parameters, and decisions are made about the types of reports that will come out of the system. Codes and tables are also defined, and file interrelationships established. In the *implementation phase,* the system is actually installed and put into operation; arrangements are made for operating, maintaining, and administering the system; and efforts are made to gain the acceptance of the users and other participants in the system.

Predesign Phase

Every company that is embarking on the design and implementation of an employee information system needs to consider its present level of systems development. Some firms have no systems at all, some have manual systems, and some use EAM-based systems in personnel activities; others have already established a few payroll-related computer-based programs. Thus any one or a combination of various conditions may exist in companies.

What motivates companies to alter their present methods? Sometimes they experience such serious problems that someone in top management says, "We need to investigate this situation to see what can be done about it." Other times, a top executive is convinced that computers and information technology should be used because they will provide the most advanced methods available. Still other times, companies adopt computer systems simply because their competitors have them. Regardless of the reason, when top management decides that a change is needed, it is likely that a group of people will be appointed to examine the situation and recommend a course of action.

Such a committee was established at Eastman Kodak Company to consider the feasibility of developing a corporatewide employee information system. The group consisted of one representative from personnel, one from systems, and one from the statistical information department. The committee members talked with a number of people about the range of problems in handling employee information and investigated how these problems might be approached. One person reports, "We tried to avoid prejudging that this would be a computer-based system. I wasn't sure what I would recommend until one member of top management came to me and indicated that he was convinced we needed a computer-based system. He said, 'It's coming, so we might as well get started.' After all, our corporate job shouldn't be one of putting out yesterday's fires, but preventing tomorrow's." Stories of this sort are commonplace. In the companies interviewed, recognition that now is the time to "get on with it," and the existence of pressing problems, caused feasibility study groups to conclude that they should develop computer-based employee information systems.

SETTING GOALS

After some initial investigation and discussion, these study groups start to define the goals they would like to accomplish with a computer-based system. These goals may be defined in terms of desired results, or they may be stated in operational terms. For example, Eastman Kodak Company set as its goals (1) elimination of duplication, (2) standardization of methods, (3) consistency of personnel data, (4) flexibility, and (5) accessibility.

Some companies have entered into the development of an employee information system with the objective of cutting costs. A few firms report success; however, most have not obtained this objective. Honeywell, Inc. reports cost savings as a result of its initial efforts to reduce duplication of reports and redundancy in data handling. Xerox Corporation, on the other hand, reports that its system development efforts were sold on the basis of availability of information, rather than cost savings. Richard T. Bueschel, president of Time Share Corporation, confirms that this is a more realistic expectation. Only 4 of 61 companies participating in a survey he conducted in 1966 reported actual dollar savings in labor costs. Mr. Bueschel states, "The benefits of using data processing in personnel seem to be largely intangible values, not direct dollar savings."[1]

The statements of other companies show additional objectives, some of which are related to activities involved in system development. For example, RCA lists immediate objectives for its personnel systems efforts —namely: (1) refinement and enhancement of routine systems to reduce volume and handling of routine data, (2) substitution of new capability provided by equipment and by uniform ways of handling data, and (3) establishment of a data-base foundation in which a dictionary of terms is a key element.

[1] Richard T. Bueschel, *EDP and Personnel*, Management Bulletin 86, American Management Association, Inc., 1966, p. 6.

Philip Morgan, of Information Science Incorporated, states operational objectives: (1) collect, organize, maintain, and store only that information you need to know, (2) establish a single source of personnel information and eliminate redundancy in handling and storage (develop a common data base), (3) establish one set of multiple-use documents for both updating and local storage of employee information, and (4) develop a powerful information-retrieval program.

Quentin Hughes, of Polaroid Corporation, says that his company defined specific immediate objectives for each of the systems efforts undertaken in its "Project Alliance."[2] He further states that success in Polaroid's program is dependent on its efforts to (1) develop an understanding of the system in the company, (2) establish confidence in the system, (3) gain acceptance of the program, and (4) create a willingness to use the system. The value of these latter objectives lies in their relationship to operational activities involved in developing employee information systems.

ESTABLISHING PRIORITIES

When a company first considers the task of developing a comprehensive personnel data system, it can easily become overwhelmed at the immensity and complexity of the job. The problem is somewhat analogous to eating an elephant—it is a big job, which is best done by taking one bite at a time. Instead of trying to do everything at once, most companies apply their initial developmental efforts to only a portion of the total information system. These first segments should be designed so that they will be compatible with the portions of the

---

[2] "How to Develop and Implement a Viable EDP Personnel System," *Employee Relations Bulletin*, Report No. 1090, March 27, 1968, pp. 11–13.

system to be developed later, but much can be gained in the total project by insuring that the first attempts, although limited, are successful. As Quentin Hughes indicates, not only will the people engaged in developing the system acquire competence, but they will also gain the confidence of others that a workable, useful system will result from their efforts.

Which application should be selected first? For the most part, this depends on the situation in which a company finds itself. In some of the companies interviewed, the possibility of developing a computer-based employee information system was considered first because of a specific problem. If at all possible, it makes sense for such companies to start on the part of a system that will help solve that problem. The need is recognized; the people who identified the problem, or who are affected by it, will be allies and support personnel's efforts; other people will be aware of what personnel is trying to do and, therefore, are likely to help personnel in every way possible. Moreover, they will be grateful when the problem is successfully solved, and thus will be more likely to support personnel in future efforts to develop the system further.

In general, companies begin their information system efforts in the areas of greatest need, or where the maximum payout will be obtained. Various companies perceive these needs and payouts differently. Historically, payroll is the first area to be considered. If companies want a smoother, more adequate system for gathering, storing, processing, and reporting payroll information, then that probably will be the first area of concern. If they already have a workable payroll system, then the attention of a preliminary study group is likely to be drawn to other types of employee information.

The second most likely area of concern is descriptive information about employees. This application may take the form of collecting and reporting data from personal profiles, work histories, or skills inventories. Personal and work history data are usually tied to a regular reporting document, such as an employee change notice, while skills inventory information is normally gathered through a questionnaire. Many firms are wary of skills inventories, and participating companies report several abortive attempts in this area. Generally, the problem stems from the company's inability to define precisely what information should be in the inventory and what will be expected of it when it is reported out. Apprehension was expressed by one executive, who said, "We don't even mention skills inventory. It scares people in this company." Yet some firms that began with this application have reported satisfaction with their results.

Other firms, such as Polaroid Corporation, begin their systems efforts in support of a specific personnel policy, such as job posting. At Polaroid, jobs are filled by posting requisitions, and previously the time lag was considered unnecessarily long. This was the first of the company's personnel applications to be computer-based. It was highly successful, so the company went on to include recruitment and then a limited manpower forecasting program. Its next effort was to develop a master file of descriptive personal data, and that was followed by the inclusion of limited skills inventory data.

As may be seen from the foregoing, selection of the first personnel application to be programmed depends largely on the specific situation. During the predesign phase it is the task of the people involved to determine which needs for employee information are most critical and which portions of an information system will produce the greatest payout so that a strategy for getting approval, and accomplishing the job, can be developed.

Management's Response and Involvement

In a number of companies, some members of top management are unenthusiastic about computer-based information systems. As it is in the expenditure of funds for any project, the burden of proof to establish the need and value of a venture is on those who propose such innovations. Since an employee information system cannot always be justified solely on the basis of cost savings, it is necessary for those people preparing such a proposal to delineate carefully the justification for the development of a system. The management and organizational considerations that affect the development and implementation of employee information systems are discussed in greater detail in the next chapter; therefore, at this point all that needs to be noted is that preliminary investigating committees need to consider the wishes and concerns of top management. A project of this magnitude requires the support of top executives, and it is not likely to succeed unless line managers agree on the worthiness of the project and offer their support during its design and implementation.

It is particularly important that members of management understand the scope and size of a proposed project since they will determine the amount of resources to be committed to the development of the system. Without adequate resources it is highly unlikely that the information system will be successful. A partial effort may be worse than no effort at all, and unsatisfied expectations resulting from inadequate budgets and capital expenditures are likely to produce frustration in managers and others who are affected by the systems effort. Such an effort is analogous to building a bridge halfway across a river.

Key Factors in Early System Design

In addition to developing strategies to gain acceptance of the system from management and others, a predesign group needs to develop some basic strategies involving the nature of the proposed system and what it should do for the company. One of these concerns the *purpose* for which information is gathered and for which it will be used. In some companies, the purpose designated by the predesign group is to provide the central office with information that will enable it to advise divisional departments and local managers. In other firms, the system is intended to facilitate centralized control of the personnel function. The two types of systems are usually very different.

Systems may be designed to take advantage of centralized data processing. Through accessing routines, geographically remote divisions can access all employee information in the central files, while the central office may be able to access only a small part of it. This factor is important when considering the *level* of the organization to be served.

Another key factor is whom the system is designed to serve—that is, the *users*. Some employee information systems primarily serve the personnel department; some primarily serve line managers; and some, both groups. Some systems are also designed to serve individual employees.

Another factor that affects strategy is the *type of system*. One company chose a single, central file for all employee information, without regard for the source of the data or who might use it. Its system was designed to gather all employee information

from one basic source document, to be put into a single file so that all users could draw employee information from the file, for any purpose whatsoever—personnel, finance, accounting, line management, payroll, and so on. One personnel man in this company expressed the thought, "We now think that it was a mistake to call this a 'personnel' system. Granted, data in the file are about people, but since the system is used by accounting, finance, and many other functions in addition to personnel, it is much more than just a personnel system."

The *timing* or speed with which new systems are introduced is another important factor. As previously noted, Richard Bueschel states that it is a mistake to duplicate mechanically what was previously done manually. This point of view is not shared by all executives. The following statement was made by an executive in another firm: "You can't get sophisticated immediately. We started with a fairly simple system, and not very good data, and then we upgraded as we went along." Leon Berg, of Xerox Corporation, comments on this seeming contradiction:

> At the beginning, the first mechanical system in a company is usually an extension of the previous manual system. Users cannot envision how to use a more sophisticated system. The second cut is usually much more sophisticated, and costs much more money.
>
> People can't stand the big change at first. For sophisticated systems you need different managers. These managers are comfortable with writing parameter cards, using simulators, phrasing questions, and so on.

Predesign groups have to assess the abilities of managers in their companies and decide how fast these managers will be able to accommodate to changes brought about by a computer-based employee information system. Only then can the groups recommend the level of sophistication that could be utilized by their particular organizations.

ORGANIZING AND STAFFING THE PROJECT

It is conceivable, but highly unlikely, that one person could do all the tasks necessary to design and implement an employee information system. These tasks are both numerous and varied, and usually include the following activities: (1) defining what the system should do and how it should operate; (2) designing the logical arrangements and relationships that will be in the system; (3) writing procedures for people to follow under the new system; (4) translating logical system requirements for data processing into machine (computer) language; (5) training people who will operate the system; (6) supervising and assisting people to put the system into operation; and (7) watching over the system after it has been installed, working out the "bugs," and insuring that the system is effective.

To do all these tasks, a person needs to be expert in the personnel function and should be able to talk fluently with personnel people and line management about their personnel responsibilities. He should have the systems man's ability to define the logical possibilities and arrangements that might evolve in the future operation of the system. He should be a programmer—that is, be conversant with machine language and have the ability to program the computer efficiently. He should know enough about the operation of the business to write workable procedures. He should be able both to train people to operate the system and to work with people throughout the company as a change agent to get the system installed. And he should be able to administer the system during its operation. Few, if any, persons have all those qualifications.

These tasks can best be shared by three or four types of people. Most task forces include an employee information specialist, a systems man, one or more programmers, and representatives from other functions that will draw information from the system. This task force may be directed or influenced primarily by either the systems man or the personnel representative. But numerous reasons are cited throughout this report that indicate the desirability of personnel's taking a strong rather than weak role in this task force.

In every company interviewed, executives emphasized that the men responsible for the design and implementation of an employee information system should be assigned to the project on a full-time basis. Persons who have been involved in such a project unanimously agree that the job cannot be performed part time, while a man is doing his regular job. L. D. Babcock, director of such a project at Walker Manufacturing Company, stated, "Anyone who is going into an EDP system should put someone in charge and let him concentrate on the personnel data system." Companies that tried to develop a new system as a part-time effort report that they had to abandon the attempt and assign men to work full time on the project.

It is difficult to generalize about the size of task forces needed to design and implement systems. Moreover, citing specific examples is not very helpful unless one knows the scope and complexity of the system that is being developed, as well as the time allotted to the job. Most of the systems observed during this study had task forces of 3 to 15 people and took from eight months to two and one-half years to complete.

Richard Bueschel, of Time Share Corporation, gives this time estimate: "Assuming you have the optimum number of people, a complete system should take eight to nine months. The longer time you take, the more organizational and operational changes will occur during the stretch-out."

Mr. Bueschel's research discloses that while a project is being conducted, approximately 15 percent of the time is spent in system analysis, 25 percent in system design, 40 percent in programming, and 20 percent in the implementation of the system. Although his time estimates seem a little optimistic when compared with the results of the author's study, Mr. Bueschel's reasoning about change is valid. For example, one company designed its employee information system for a centralized organization; but, by the time the project was in the implementation phase, the company had decentralized. Since the system did not fit the new organization very well, many changes had to be made. Most of the companies interviewed during this study acknowledged that they underestimated the time, number of people, and cost required to complete a system.

The task force of a systems project is made up of people from different parts of a company. The employee information specialist is usually a man with considerable personnel experience. Most companies rely on their computer departments to provide the necessary systems and programming support. However, one company reports that, because of a shortage of systems men, it selected men from its personnel statistics department and trained them to do systems work. Persons from other functions that are closely related to, or affected by, the employee information system may also be members of the task force or will work with the group as required.

Some companies report that they used consultants to help them during the pre-design and design phases of the project. One executive states:

Because of their previous experience, consultants have capabilities that we don't

have. They can play an important role in the definition of systems, more so than in the personnel aspects of a program. They offer alternatives that we wouldn't ordinarily think of, and they add weight to arguments when we present them to management.

Design Phase

Before designing a new employee information system, most companies study or analyze the content and flow of their present personnel information. The purpose of this analysis is to determine the content of information collected by each form, where each element of information is captured originally, the flow of forms, where this information is used, what approvals are required, and so on. Companies making this type of analysis are impressed with the duplication of data, as well as with how uninformed people are about the origin and use of information in their company.

Philip Morgan, of Information Science, reports that over 30 large company studies conducted by his firm show that the personnel function uses an average of 230 forms, or approximately 1,500 to 2,000 data elements, of which only 190 to 210 are unduplicated items. Most companies use a matrix sheet to display data elements and the forms on which they appear. Data elements are arranged in the matrix so that one can see the scope and pattern of information that is presently in the information system. This technique can also be used to establish the cost of the present system. (A portion of a matrix is illustrated in Exhibit 12.)

WHAT SHOULD THE SYSTEM LOOK LIKE?

The next job is to define the outlines and details of an information system. This definition of the general system will include

EXHIBIT 12. *Information Matrix Sheet*

Report Name and Number															
EMPLOYEE INFORMATION ITEMS															
1 Employee number															
2 Check sort															
3 Payroll type															
4 Employee class															
5 Status															
6 Turnover or terminating date															
7 Terminating type															
8 Location state															
9 Location city															
10 Current labor grade															
11 Nonhourly pay-period rate															
12 Shift															
13 Department number															
14 Federal income tax code															
15 Current overtime rate															
16 Current hourly rate															
17 Monthly salary															
18 Life insurance deduction amount															
19 United fund deduction amount															
20 Bond deduction amount															
21 Dependent hospital ins. effective date															
22 Leave date															
23 Leave-return date															
24 Birth date															

objectives, data sources, number and frequency of outputs, data files and their sizes, a proposed schedule of operations, and interrelation with other systems. It will also include a system flow chart, a description of data elements, a description of inputs, a description of outputs, and methods and procedures for data processing. All this results in a document called a systems definition.

The Ford Motor Company reports that its people went to the divisions four times and asked for suggestions. Then they designed a system and drew up a description of it, which they routed to the divisions. After getting the divisions' responses, they adjusted the system description. This procedure of checking with future systems users is of critical importance. Saul Citrone, of IBM, states, "Before I do anything in designing a system or data bank I require the users to define what they want, and what they want to do with the information." If a system is to be successful, it must be user-effective—that is, it must be capable of doing what the users want it to do.

During the design phase many decisions are made that will affect the final nature of the system. Some firms rely primarily on a standard dictionary of terms or on central file maintenance to provide system compatibility among their divisions. Some companies use "explosive file maintenance" to insure consistency, while others change each data element in the file separately. Explosive file maintenance is accomplished within the computer—when one item is changed, all other items related to it, or affected by it, are changed automatically. With the other technique, a related data item can be changed only when an entry is made for it. Some systems have the capacity to update each record individually, while others require "passing the entire file" during each file maintenance. The possibilities are numerous, but the foregoing may suggest the diversity and complexity of design considerations.

WHAT INFORMATION IS NEEDED?

In an effort to determine what information is needed by members of management for their decision making, system designers often ask them to express their opinions about the data they are now using. In general, this approach has not been very effective. In talking with executives, most systems designers refer to company objectives, bylaws, policy statements, procedures, and legal requirements. Some systems designers talk with executives about the information they now receive, but do not ask them to define their information needs. Other designers use a "paucity of data" approach, leaving the burden of proof on the manager to justify his need for the information. If there is a demonstrable reason, the information is included.

Another key question is the degree of accuracy needed. Must data be 100 percent accurate, or will 99 percent do? "Accuracy costs money," says one executive, "and if you are willing to pay for it, it can be achieved." Companies have found that capturing information from manually maintained personnel jackets seldom, or never, results in accurate, up-to-date information. Some firms use questionnaires for the original input of data and then check their files with employees after the original file records have been created. Most firms report that accurate information can best be obtained from normally processed routine documents, such as employee-change notices, coupled with a strict edit-and-audit routine performed automatically by the computer.

Although input and update parameters have already been discussed, one further comment on outputs is necessary. At Honeywell, the employee information specialist prepared a manual on the reports to be produced from the system. He listed every report coming from the system, along with a full justification for each. The manual shows the origin of data for each report, reporting path, report formats, users of each report, decisions for which information is necessary, and copies of any special forms required to collect or report data. This type of report manual is used by other companies. Although it is time consuming to create, it is valuable because it helps systems designers think through the purpose and use of information.

Some firms find it advantageous to tie internal data collection to the reporting of company data to some external agency. For example, the collection of data for a report to corporate headquarters is tied to the tax-reporting cycle; divisions must submit data at specified times so that they can be aggregated for tax reports. This relationship gives leverage and increases both the timeliness and accuracy of data. A variation of this method is arranging to feed the payroll file from the personnel file, if the two files are separate. Since great efforts are made to keep the payroll accurate and to process it on time, similar efforts can be applied when the personnel system is tied to it.

Implementation Phase

Converting information technology from manual to computer systems is difficult because it affects work routines, organization, and ways of thinking and managing. It also requires a different, more rigorous discipline on the part of those who operate the information system. The design and implementation of an employee information system require thinking through all the possibilities that might affect the system sometime in the future. Because this re-

quirement is the chief enemy, as well as the chief value, of developing and installing a new system, it is necessary to make special efforts to gain acceptance of the system prior to its inception.

Few firms use force in trying to gain acceptance of systems; instead, they attempt to sell the systems on the basis of need by or benefit to potential users. Some companies wait until the need is pointed out by the line organization, while others rely on the personnel department to emphasize the need for, or value of, a new information system. Usually, need is most apparent when manual systems of collecting information or producing reports take too long or are too difficult to process. At such times managers are usually very receptive to changes in the information system. Whatever the reason, acceptance and support, they are needed from those people in the organization who will operate, or be affected by, the new system.

INSTALLING AN EMPLOYEE INFORMATION SYSTEM

An executive of a large Eastern manufacturing corporation describes his company's installation of an employee information system as follows:

First, we got acceptance of all major projects from top management and the highest personnel executives. Second, we reviewed the tentative system definition with each personnel director, and formed a task force to implement the system. This task force was a necessary communication link since it had to determine when the system did not meet local needs. It also had to install the system. Third, the task force wrote a review of how local needs would be met, and it reviewed and approved the dictionary of terms. Fourth, we picked a pilot plant, installed the system, and debugged it. We ran the new system parallel with the old, manual system for a fixed period of time before discontinuing the old system. After the system has operated successfully in one plant, we plan to install it in several other plants more or less simultaneously.

An executive of a Midwestern manufacturing company reports the following process:

First we tried to generate personnel information from our payroll system. But we found that it was not accurate, since much of the personnel data didn't directly affect payroll activities and had not been kept current. When we ran reports from these data, management rejected them as worthless.

So we set up a separate program. First we collected data by questionnaire and added [them] to our data base. Next we created a job history data base and conceptualized our validation and file-maintenance programs. In the next phase, we programmed our new payroll system and fit it to our employee change-notice procedures. We then added salary history to our data base.

In the beginning, over 90 percent of the incoming employee change notices had errors of one kind or another. These have been corrected; and today the error rate is almost negligible.

Another large firm reports that the most important thing in installing a system is that the company do a thorough training job, developing almost routine performance and full knowledge on the part of those who will operate the system. "This is worth the effort it takes," says one of the executives. This firm makes a concerted effort to get suggestions from foremen and others so that they will be involved in the systems effort.

At Ford Motor Company, an excellent programmed instruction booklet was given to all secretaries who might be involved in preparing and submitting inputs to the sys-

tem. Most firms echo the need for, and the importance of, training. In installing a timekeeping system in St. Louis, McDonnell Douglas utilized handouts, a 20-minute training film, and group training sessions for those supervisors and their assistants who would be affected by the new system. The trainers encouraged participants to ask questions about any points that were not clear, on the premise that "If we don't answer them here, we'll have to answer them on the floor when the system is installed." (The company found that more questions were asked when only one level of supervision was in the room at any given time.)

At training sessions held by U.S. Plywood-Champion Papers, Inc., particular attention was paid to attitudes among personnel representatives from remote locations. "We tried to show what we were doing and why, and what they could gain from the system," reports an executive. "We tried to show that just because we were dealing with numbers didn't mean that they would become only numbers in the company." This concern about attitudes is reflected in the statement of another executive charged with installing a system: "You've got to involve those people who are in the jobs affected by the development of the system; otherwise, it becomes your system instead of their system."

The process of installing an employee information system is not a very smooth one, judging from reports gathered during this research. Procedural changes, an integral part of the process, always present problems. Conversion of information from manual files, or the initial collection of information from people by questionnaires, is likely to spring many surprises on systems designers, who are supposed to anticipate all possibilities. Auditing data to weed out incorrect information and getting it corrected are processes that demand infinite detail and patience. More than likely, errors discovered in machine programs will also have to be corrected.

It is during the installation process that all the previously established groundwork pays off. If top management has given its support, if system analysis has been thorough, if system design has been carefully selected, if machine programs have been meticulously prepared, if procedures have been detailed correctly, and if training has been sound, then the information system may be installed successfully, without any great trauma for the organization.

Administering a System

The previous description slightly idealizes the developmental process. In reality, the people involved are probably not sure that programs will run, inputs will arrive, and reports will be produced; and they may even suspect that major parts of the system will "blow up" during the first few processing cycles. Moreover, in a large system this process of system installation has to be carried out for every single module. Very often companies have several modules at different stages of development. When one part of the system works adequately, another part becomes the focal point of those responsible for developing the system. However, once a portion of the system has been installed, it must be administered and certain activities must be performed on a continuing basis.

Administering an employee information system involves many activities, but the major ones are as follows:

1. Monitoring daily activities against the system; insuring that inputs arrive and are in proper condition for processing; receiving reports from computer operations, insuring the correctness of their forms and sending them to their respective destinations; receiving requests for special reports to be generated and insuring that they are produced; tracking down any errors that appear in reports or inputs; and solving any problems that may arise in procedural aspects of the system.

2. Responding to changes in the organization or changes in information that necessitate a change in machine programs. Making small changes with a programmer, and larger ones with the help of a systems man.

3. Working with users of the system to develop new ways of using information in order to make the system more valuable to the company.

4. Handling any interfaces with other related systems.

Companies find that it is advisable to try to centralize or in some way control daily activities against the system, as well as to try to limit changes that may be effected against it. One way of accomplishing this monitoring is through the use of a personnel information center to process routine data and a personnel systems man to control changes in the system. Another method is assigning an employee information specialist to control and monitor all activities against the system, with routine processing performed through local employee information representatives.

At Standard Oil Company (Ohio) staff members of the personnel information centers perform the following activities:

1. Review all personnel action forms.
2. Process all performance appraisal information.
3. Process skills-inventory documents.
4. Keep invention agreements and confidential documents.
5. Review an exception listing of an end-of-the-month computer comparison of payroll and employee relations

tapes to insure consistency of records.

6. Process reports going to department heads and staff groups.

7. Process any requests for normal and routine computer-processed reports and insure the "need to know" of the recipient.

In addition to the personnel information centers, Standard Oil (Ohio) has an information development and systems support staff that coordinates all systems work within the personnel function. This staff also reviews in general all machine programs for accuracy and effectiveness. Nonroutine report requests that require programming, or program changes to existing programs, must be approved by the manager, employee relations information systems. New systems and programs of major proportions, such as programs for the new employee relations management information system, must be approved by the general manager of the MIS project.

Philip Morgan, of Information Sciences, says the value of a personnel information center is that it consolidates responsibility for review of incoming data, for reports, and for contact with systems. The purpose of this arrangement is to provide a single source of information and a firm, known responsibility for all aspects of the employee information system.

The second, closely related method of controlling an employee information system is through an employee information specialist. This method is used by Honeywell, with a person designated as specialist in the design, implementation, and administration of an employee information system. The specialist's activities are described at Honeywell as follows:

1. Act as a representative of the using managers. The employee information specialist will not be under the dom-

ination of the manager who produces data at the computer center.

2. Work with managers to help determine their employee information needs.

3. Take inventory of present employee information systems.

4. Conduct work-simplification studies to establish more efficient ways of handling personnel information.

5. Develop new uses for data. The employee information specialist has to understand users' needs, convince them to use the system, gain acceptance of reports, and get users to rely more fully on the system.

6. Help managers develop new horizons regarding potential information uses; develop their involvement and concern for how data are produced.

7. Set up, and work with, a council of employee information specialists. Each division will have a representative, and this council will handle interfaces between the corporate office and divisions.

At Honeywell each divisional office may have a local personnel information center under the functional supervision of the divisional employee information specialist. This center handles routine activities similar to those of Standard Oil (Ohio). But the key person in the system is the employee information specialist. His job starts when the system is in the first stages of design and continues during its implementation and throughout its administration. The major purpose of the specialist's job is to educate as well as to control. (Exhibit 13 is a diagram of the relationship between the employee information specialist and other members of Honeywell's organization.)

Even though a company has neither a personnel information center nor an employee information specialist, it must per-

EXHIBIT 13. *Relationship Between the Employee Information Specialist and the Organization: Developmental and Operational Phases (Honeywell Inc.)*

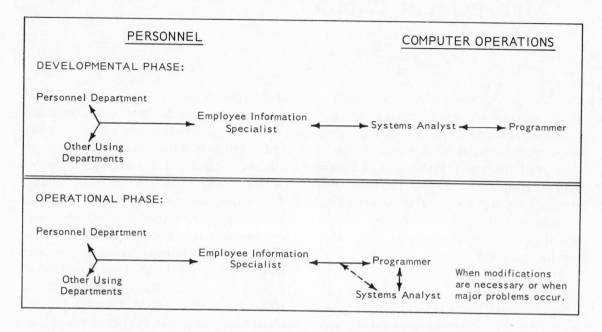

form the same activities as other firms. It may or may not perform them in the same way, but frequently the organizational arrangements are similar, although the groups and specialists have different titles. Usually, there is a systems man to handle day-to-day problems, as well as new developments in the system. Sometimes he is on the personnel staff and sometimes in the systems department, with the employee information system assigned to him. And, usually, there is a person in the personnel office whose main job is concerned with personnel data; he may have the title "personnel systems specialist" or something similar. In the programming group, there is generally a specific programmer with maintenance responsibility for personnel programs. And in most firms there is an office that more or less acts as a switching point for system inputs and outputs. A major difference between these arrangements is the extent of control, as well as the emphasis that is placed upon

certain other aspects of the system, such as education.

A final factor to be considered in policing the system is keeping the information "clean." Final responsibility for accurate information rests with the user, since the manager who inputs the information also receives the reports. However, the personnel information center, the employee information specialist, and the personnel systems man are also involved. The center is in an excellent position to monitor data. The information specialist and the personnel systems man are able to monitor the system from a key position, and they can work with the programmer in solving minor problems in data processing. Obviously, one of the chief concerns is to make the system as valuable to the company as possible. Reliability and completeness of information are key variables in determining whether an information system will be worthwhile.

4. The Effects of Organizational and Management Factors

WHEN PERSONNEL EXECU-tives first consider developing a computer-based employee information system, they often examine what other companies have done, with the hope that they will find some systems that can be adapted for their own needs. They also turn to companies selling computers and computer software to find out if they have ready-made programs that can be purchased.

For most of the companies interviewed during this study, this hope was not realized. Although their personnel executives were helped by learning what others were doing, each of these companies had to develop its own system to meet its own particular requirements. But whether a company tries to adapt another firm's application for its use or designs its own system, a number of significant questions must be answered before the project can begin. Still other questions always emerge before the project is brought to fruition.

During this study it became apparent that, although there are many similarities between the personnel information systems of companies, there are also tremendous differences. Such similarities and differences between companies are prevalent in many types of systems—accounting, marketing, production, and other programs. In the development of computer-based systems, however, companies need to identify and analyze the organizational and management factors to be served, before the systems are designed and implemented.

The type of employee information system developed by a company is the result of interplay between a large number of factors. Some of these factors are organizational; for example, the size of the company and the degree of decentralization are critical. Also important are the various styles of management practiced in the company. Top management attitudes regarding computers and information systems affect the development of personnel systems. Personnel department philosophy, objectives, and policies affect the kind of employee information desired and determine the ways in which it will be collected and used. Finally, relationships between the personnel department and systems people in the company, and relationships between the personnel department and the line organization, are also critical factors in designing and implementing an employee information system.

Organizational Factors

A manufacturer operating only one large plant will have information systems quite different from those of a company with many plants throughout the country. In addition to the variables of company size and geographic location, the level and location of decision centers play an important part in designing an information system, as does the nature of the relationship between corporate and divisional groups. The rate of organizational change experienced by a firm often affects information needs, just as it affects the availability of resources that can be allocated to meet the information needs of a personnel department.

Size

The present survey discloses that companies ranging from 300 employees to more than 300,000 employees have EDP applications in the personnel function. A previous regional survey found that companies with as few as 100 employees had applications in personnel.*

In the present study, questionnaires and interviews confirm that computer-based personnel applications tend to be more complex and greater in scope in large companies than in small firms. This is what one would expect, since size leads to complexity, as well as to a need for more formal methods of collecting and filing data about people. Larger companies tend to have larger personnel departments, with more specialization of function and, apparently in some cases, bigger budgets. In any event, large organizational size seems to force personnel departments to deal with some problems that just cannot be ignored. For example, in firms with only a few hundred employees, the personnel man usually can obtain limited personnel data from other people if such data are mandatory; however, in firms with 20,000 or more employees, the personnel department may find obtaining accurate data in this way impossible.

Large companies and small firms have a number of similar problems. They compete in national labor markets; they share an interest in efficient administration; and they both need some control of the personnel function. In addition, smaller firms have some of the same capacity to develop computer-based employee information systems as large companies.

As mentioned earlier, the survey data collected during this study disclosed no direct correlation between the size of a company

---

* Edward J. Morrison, "EDP Applications in Personnel in Selected Colorado Businesses," *Colorado Business Review,* June 1967, pp. 3–7.

and the degree of sophistication or number of its EDP applications in personnel. Several companies with 10,000 to 20,000 employees were found to have computer-based personnel applications far more complex and extensive than companies twice their size. Two of the major determining factors seemed to be top management's enthusiasm about management information systems and the strong dedication of people in the personnel department to having a mechanized employee information system.

Degree of Decentralization

The companies that were interviewed represent a broad spectrum of organizational arrangements. In some, decision making is primarily centralized; others have highly autonomous branches, divisions, or companies within their structures. Some of the companies are geographically centralized, while others are spread throughout the country, or even the world. In some companies, divisions differ in their organizational relationships with the corporate group because their products differ or because some of them were purchased as subsidiary companies. Other divisions are highly unionized, which creates a different set of information needs.

In companies where divisions have autonomy of operation, their personnel practices are quite dissimilar, and computer configurations are sometimes widely different, or perhaps even nonexistent in some divisions. In other companies there is little difference between the personnel practices of various divisions, even though they have developed independently, with little or no attempt made to standardize or coordinate them. Obviously, broad variations in the policies and practices of a company's divisions create problems if a common employee information system is imposed on all of them.

Although some of the participating companies find that their decentralized units independently arrived at fairly homogeneous manual systems during a period of time, other firms report that personnel departments in some of their divisions developed rather advanced computer-based programs and applications before corporate efforts in this area were begun. Some companies report that these divisions are reluctant to adopt a corporate-inspired-and-designed system, which to them looks no better, or perhaps even worse, than the ones that they themselves developed.

In all the foregoing situations, two basic questions relating to decentralization and systems are implicit: (1) At which level, and by whom, are decisions to be made? (2) At which level in the organization should various data be made available for decision-making and audit purposes? There are almost as many answers to these questions as there are organizations attempting to design employee information systems.

RELATIONSHIP BETWEEN CORPORATE STAFF AND DIVISIONS

All the companies interviewed during this study have corporate offices and several divisions. As might be expected, no single organizational strategy is followed by all these firms; however, executives in all of them agree that relationships between their corporate offices and divisional groups play an important role in the design and implementation of corporatewide systems. Some of the typical arrangements that were observed among these companies are as follows:

1. Centralized planning, administration, and control of corporatewide functions, such as personnel.
2. Corporate control of broad policy and corporate administration of some specific services or programs, such as employee benefits, with decentralized administration and control of most personnel programs.
3. Corporate influence on broad policy and divisional responsibility for program design, administration, and control.

The task of designing an employee information system, securing approval for its inception, and implementing it would be quite dissimilar under each of these arrangements.

Many companies report considerable difficulty in trying to change established patterns of conducting personnel programs in their divisions. They have experienced numerous problems in attempting to institute uniform, corporatewide data processing methods and information systems. While some firms express satisfaction with their progress in overcoming these problems, others do not try to overcome them; they choose an alternative route instead. For example, rather than requiring divisions to conform to a standard operating system, the companies require only standard inputs to the corporate system from the divisions and in turn provide them with standard outputs. Other companies settle for the degree of uniformity that can be obtained by issuing a standard dictionary of terms and data-element configuration to all the divisions. Beyond that, the companies let each division design and operate its own system as it wishes.

Companies also differ in the methods they use to get divisions on board when new systems are initiated. One method is for the corporate group to design a new system and then impose it on the entire company by a top management directive. Fortunately, this approach is seldom used. A second method is to design the system at corporate headquarters, with or without the help of divisions, and then sell it to the divisions. A third method is to design the system at corporate headquarters and then wait until division managers experience problems, which usually arise as a result of organizational growth or change. Then corporate staff specialists show the division managers how the information system can help them resolve their problems.

In each of the participating companies, the methods used to implement employee information systems were influenced by past company practices, the status and power of the corporate group, the extent of top management's commitment to information concepts, and management's characteristic style of managing change.

ORGANIZATIONAL CHANGE

Several of the companies interviewed were undergoing rapid growth and change during the time they were developing and implementing their employee information systems. Some companies report that they are growing beyond their old systems' capacities to maintain centralized control, and they are in the process of decentralizing decision making. One firm had between 15,000 and 20,000 employees, and at one time its average length of employee service was little more than one year! The requirements of this firm's employee information system are quite different from those imposed on the system of a firm with a highly stable workforce and growth pattern.

The companies experiencing rapid growth report that their manual systems got overloaded and broke down. Several executives stated that companies can get along quite well with EAM (electronic accounting machine) applications in personnel and payroll, so long as the organization is not too large and the range of questions requiring answers is not too broad or is not subject to change. But growth, complexity, and change tend to make manual and EAM systems obsolete. Moreover, the survey showed, as

some firms grew, the members of management seemed to place less emphasis on the art of management and more on the science of decision making and began to concentrate on the measurement of results against predetermined objectives.

Personnel executives in one company observe that their firm is changing from a small, informal, centrally controlled organization to a large, depersonalized, bureaucratic, decentralized organization. Persons trying to design computer-based information systems in this company state that as yet management does not seem to know just what its information needs are. In newly decentralized organizations, the patterns of decision making take time to evolve and stabilize. This observation is reported in most companies that are undergoing rapid growth or change in management strategy or organizational structure.

Several of the systems people interviewed agree that organizations in a state of change should design and implement very flexible systems. Usually, this implies a modular approach, with parts of the information system small enough to permit changing them without great expense, but with all modules of the system designed so they can interact with each other mechanically.

*Management Attitudes
Regarding Systems*

In some companies, executives seem content with their present reporting methods and control mechanisms and are not actively seeking to replace them with new, expensive management information systems. Either the executives may be satisfied with the results obtained from their present reporting methods, or they may feel so comfortable with these methods that they are reluctant to change; but in either case there is little desire to revamp the information systems being used. By contrast, executives in other companies are definitely dissatisfied, either because the present methods are unsatisfactory or because they will not meet the companies' future needs. In many of these firms, efforts are being made to establish new information systems and to use more advanced information technology, sometimes at considerable expense and with the commitment of sizable resources.

TOP MANAGEMENT INTEREST IN SYSTEMS

Not all top managers are impressed with the current interest in and emphasis on EDP-based management information systems. Some companies are proceeding very slowly and cautiously, while others seem to be strongly committed to rapid development and implementation of management information systems throughout the organization. Some companies, such as RCA, have policies stating that managers should fully exploit the use of management information systems for decision making. They have even conducted courses to inform managers about this developing technology. In such companies, personnel executives who are interested in developing computer-based employee information systems find a supportive climate and sometimes even an insistence that efforts be made in that direction.

This environment is quite different from that found in companies in which executives are suspicious of machine-produced data, statistical analysis, and management dependence upon systems and computers. This attitude was expressed by one division director: "I don't want my umbilical cord tied to a computer!" He will be fed information in some other way.

Information systems, like any other technological innovation, are bound to have many proponents and opponents. Both sides have strong arguments by which they justify their prejudices and feelings. The potential rewards of systems are great and their shortcomings are often obvious. Technological changes and new demands on management require the development of new skills and disciplines, but these are often threatening to the people involved. Furthermore, the costs of developing and implementing computer-based management information systems are quite often very large.

CONDITIONS FOR INNOVATION

Top management establishes the ground rules for innovation in systems and information technology. Some companies foster rapid change, try new methods, and encourage people to develop new ideas and find new solutions to old (and new) problems. Receptiveness to innovation is expressed by comments such as: "You can try anything once." "Anything goes. Just don't fail too often." "This organization is committed to new ideas." Other companies make changes more slowly.

In addition to differences in the pace at which change is introduced, the methods used by companies to bring about changes often vary considerably. Personnel executives interested in developing computer-based employee information systems necessarily operate according to their own particular organizational environments. For example, one way in which Eli Lilly & Company makes an effort to gain acceptance, as Richard Brown, director of personnel planning, explains:

In some instances, people have to develop their need for something new. Sometimes, if you want them to accept changes, you should plant the seed of a new way of doing things, and let the seed grow. People are often uncomfortable with theories. In order to get a new concept accepted, sometimes one must point out existing situations, wait for problems to be recognized, and then propose systems that can answer these problems.

MANAGEMENT'S COST ORIENTATION

When a commitment to change is coupled with a commitment to improve decision making, the next consideration is obtaining the necessary funds.

Richard Brown emphasizes that, in selling systems, top management's cost orientation can be an important factor. Corporate executives often think of funds allocated for developing computer-based information systems as an input/output arrangement—dollars expended for dollars returned or saved. This orientation is not always applicable since some systems' inputs and outputs cannot be quantified until after the fact and others are not directly measurable in dollars and cents, but result in subjective benefits.

Alex Telischak, senior vice president, Xerox Corporation, says that this problem is not insurmountable: "We should measure whatever we can measure. Sometimes it is only the cost of a system that can be measured, not its outputs." He states further that, in presenting alternatives to top management, one should indicate, "You get this unmeasurable value for this definable cost, and you get this additional undefinable value for this additional cost." Then, says Mr. Telischak, "You let executives decide what they want, select those alternatives that they think are most desirable, with an understanding of the costs involved. Executives apply their subjective judgment to the subjective portions of decisions, with an explicit understanding of the measurable costs of their selections."

Personnel Policies, Objectives, and Procedures

Companies vary in the way they treat employees, and some of them develop a distinct way of conceptualizing their relationships with employees. Robert Jones, vice president of personnel, U.S. Plywood-Champion Papers Inc., states that in most companies the personnel function does essentially what top management wants it to do. Don Garns, corporate employee information specialist and previously a personnel manager at Honeywell, Inc., agrees that personnel serves the wishes of the management team and translates these wishes into programs that reflect top management's values relating to people. Personnel executives are often selected because they are in agreement with the basic personnel policies of the company.

POLICIES AND OBJECTIVES

When an employee information system is designed and implemented, it must serve the basic personnel policies and objectives of the company. Some firms try to maintain personal contact with employees and, therefore, avoid rigorous systems, both manual and machine-based. Other companies, such as Honeywell, believe that the best way to insure that people are treated as individuals is by developing computer-based employee information systems. Gerry Morse, Honeywell's vice president, employee relations, says:

> Only by giving the routine tasks of personnel management to the computer can we get the time to return to the management part of personnel management—the job of counseling line managers in personnel matters. The computer makes it possible to analyze every personnel transaction according to any number of criteria specified by management, on an automatic schedule, every time any action is taken. Thus, in a very large company, we are able to provide a degree of personal treatment that is otherwise available only in very small companies.

The design of an employee information system is shaped by numerous policies, and its operation is affected by related procedures. When the capability desired of a system is being determined, the following policies and procedures need to be considered:

- Absences.
- Vacations.
- Clearances.
- Probationary periods.
- Transfers.
- Promotions (from within).
- Management development.
- Special groups.
- Employee benefits.
- Wages and salaries.
- Timekeeping and labor changes.
- Layoffs.
- Job posting.
- Hiring for replacement and growth.
- Recruitment.

In the companies studied, each of the above policies and procedures was observed to be a major determinant of an application in the system of one firm or another. In some cases, all the data required to routinely administer a policy were being processed by machine. Not only can systems be designed and implemented to administer daily activities in all these areas, but, in addition, the activities can be controlled by either machine audit or management decision rules that are inserted into the computer before daily transactions are processed.

In some of the companies studied, personnel executives were involved in organization planning and corporate planning. Although it seems natural for the personnel department to do this work in some companies, in others it would be inappropriate, and the personnel people's competence to plan would be questioned by executives in other departments. Certainly, employee information systems contain much of the data needed for rigorous organization planning, and personnel departments that have such systems are well qualified to conduct organizational studies. In the final analysis, however, the people most capable and best qualified to do organization planning will gain the respect of top management and will be given the job.

MAJOR FOCUS OF PERSONNEL SYSTEMS

The design of employee information systems usually reflects the emphasis a company places on specific personnel activities. At U.S. Plywood-Champion Papers, the initial systems effort supported wage and salary administration. At McDonnell Douglas, one major portion of the employee information system supports storing and processing employee records, and another part supports timekeeping and labor reporting. Polaroid set up its system to facilitate its job-posting program, which is paramount in the company. At Standard Oil (Ohio) a major concern is administration of the management development program. Part of Mobil Oil's systems effort is an advanced program to identify high-potential management people, while IBM's effort is a system to manage human resources as they progress throughout the entire company. Some people at IBM suggest that employees could use the employee information system by plugging in to search for certain kinds of data, such as job openings, at their own locations.

At none of the companies are the aforementioned applications the sole or the major functions served by the employee information system. They are mentioned only to illustrate some logical entry points into the system and the range of possibilities that exist for personnel managers who accept the challenge of systems development.

Personnel executives have to decide what they want a system to do for them, the personnel department, other departments, and the company as a whole. Three major types of configurations were observed during this research study:

1. Administration and control of personnel activities.
2. Support of management decision making.
3. Management-science applications, such as simulation and modeling.

Since all three types of applications require a data base, its development is usually one of the first major projects undertaken. At this stage, some firms are willing to settle for mass printouts of data that must be reduced manually to provide information. The next phase often involves developing more sophisticated generators for reporting data to management, including the capability to interrogate the files for answers to successively complex questions. Programming extensive edit and audit routines into normal data processing permits a company to augment its administration and control. Regular, automated file maintenance then takes over a considerable portion of the previous manual control of daily activities. Advanced management-science applications permit the company to build models of parts of the organization or aspects of the personnel function to determine the possible effects of policy alternatives before selecting the most appropriate one for the firm. Obviously, significant expense is involved in moving from one of these basic approaches to the next.

Most participating companies have systems that are oriented toward records and status changes, locating people to fill vacancies, and administering a few key policies, such as absences or wage and salary. Some firms have rather sophisticated report generators that enable management to apply extensive selection criteria to extract data from the files, and several have rather sophisticated mathematical ability to treat selected data. A number of firms have the ability to audit and control functional activities with the computer, although the range of functions controlled in this way is not yet extensive. Very few of the companies have management-science applications. Although the range of applications developed by the participating companies is broad, the potential for further development and sophistication is so much broader that it staggers the imagination. One is reminded of air transportation as it was perceived during the 1920's.

PROBLEM AREAS

Every company studied asked these questions:

- Do we need computer-based personnel information systems?
- If so, what types and how extensive should they be?
- How fast should we develop them?
- How quickly can our organization adjust to changes resulting from the systems?
- How quickly can our managers learn to use this tool?

Interviews with executives disclosed a variety of opinions about these subjects.

Some companies question the propriety of moving toward computer-based personnel systems. They want to preserve the personal touch in relationships with employees, they try to avoid impersonality, and they believe that the best way to manage people is with feelings, rather than logic. Other companies maintain that this dichotomy is false, that both logic and feelings should be applied to personnel problems, and that both personal contact and computer processing of data are legitimate and helpful. As mentioned previously, Gerry Morse, of Honeywell, thinks that the computer's ability to handle vast amounts of data, with minute inspection of every factor according to any complexity of inspection criteria specified by management, puts into our grasp the capability to personalize and individualize the treatment of employees. In his opinion, machines can do some things much better than men; therefore, these tasks should be relegated to the machine. Other tasks, more germane to management, can be performed better by men, so men should be released from routine tasks to concentrate on those activities in which they excel and those that machines cannot do at all.

Another problem mentioned by personnel executives is that large inputs to a system yield relatively small outputs. H. M. Wisely, vice president of industrial relations, Eli Lilly & Company, expresses concern about this problem in executive selection. He states that obtaining enough information to decide conclusively about candidates for a job requires a system of tremendous scope—in file size, data input, and cost of operation. By comparison, says Dr. Wisely, the output of the system seems rather small, and he questions whether his company can afford to make such a large investment for such a small output, at least at this time.

This particular concern is expressed by executives in many other companies, as evidenced by the fact that few of them rely solely on machine-processed data to make decisions about personnel matters. Most companies develop files that will help them locate high-potential candidates for a position; but, when they make a decision, the information they use is obtained from different sources. This general pattern is followed in many other areas: The computer file is used to point up potential opportunities, or problems, and then other sources of information are used for decision making.

Although this approach is not unsound, it does raise the question how far a computer-based system should go toward providing information to clarify alternative routes of action in problem solving. With the present state of management thinking and systems development, the output does not always seem to justify the great cost of inputs required to facilitate extensive applications. Part of the difficulty may be inadequate definition of alternative uses and applications to other problems. Information that serves only one area may not be worth gathering and storing; only if it can serve several areas of decision making may the cost be justified.

Timing is a critical problem in employee information systems development. Some companies take a rather casual approach, while others are moving as fast as possible into this area. As indicated previously, a major factor in the speed of developing systems seems to be the adequacy of present systems to meet information needs defined by management. Timing is also determined by management's willingness to bear the cost of developing new information systems, as well as by management's convictions about the short-term and the long-term importance of information systems in general.

One additional complication, highlighted by Gerry Morse, of Honeywell, is that computer-based information systems are sometimes considered a threat because they make demands on managers that were not made previously. Mr. Morse summarizes the reaction of personnel managers as follows: "Some managers will stand the gaff, and others will not." In some companies, managers who choose to resist using the computer, when it is available and perhaps even mandatory, find that a system can be more than a threat—it can be a potential downfall. Managers who resist change are soon identified as unpromotable.

Departmental and Group Relationships

Because of the discipline of the computer, and the cost of programming, each aspect of the entire system must be worked out in detail before initial attempts are made to program or operate the system. However, design and implementation of an employee information system never occur in a vacuum. They cannot be performed by the personnel department alone, but require close interaction between the personnel people, staff specialists, and various line and staff departments.

Each of these groups has its own special knowledge and its own part to play in the design and implementation of an employee information system. Of necessity, they must work together closely to make decisions and resolve conflicts of objectives, policies, procedures, workloads, timing, and other details inherent in a system. How this interaction occurs and the success it achieves depend largely upon the working relationships that exist before the project is begun.

PERSONNEL AND LINE

One personnel man, in charge of designing and implementing a system, reports that in his company the personnel department was a low-status function and was neither trusted nor respected by the line people. Before he could make any headway in developing a system, his group had to prove itself worthy of respect and consideration. His counterpart in another firm says that he did not have this problem; his peo-

ple went to work without any preliminaries, and without having to demonstrate their competence. But in every company interviewed, personnel executives in charge of design and implementation of employee information systems stress the importance of having, or developing, sound working relationships with line managers, who have to support the system if it is to work effectively.

In some companies, top personnel executives are part of the management team, concerned with the cost-effectiveness of· their programs and closely involved in the management of the entire company. In other organizations, personnel executives are more concerned with the well-being of employees than with economic factors and management's prerogatives, and they often have the reputation of being happiness boys filled with wild ideas. The two types of personnel departments have to work differently in designing and implementing their systems.

Another major difference is the basic purpose underlying systems development. In some personnel departments the systems serve line managers in their personnel activities, while in others they serve the personnel department. Naturally, the line managers' response to systems development is quite different in each of these cases.

PERSONNEL AND SYSTEMS

Similar problems exist in the relationship between the personnel department and the systems group. Personnel people are often considered unqualified to handle data in a rigorous manner. From the point of view of the systems people, it is up to personnel to prove this impression erroneous. As mentioned previously, personnel often gets little support in this effort from payroll groups.

A common complaint about the relationship between personnel and systems is that the systems people tend to take over projects, dictating what will be in the system and how the system will operate. Personnel executives also complain that systems people design systems that, while mechanically sound and efficient, are not very effective in serving the personnel needs of line managers and the personnel department. For their part, systems people often report that they wish personnel were more demanding and competent and that, when personnel does not take an active role, systems people have to make things work as well as they can. Several personnel men report that, if they were to participate in a project again, they would take a much stronger role than in the past. Obviously, the selection of competent personnel men is of key importance.

In some companies the personnel function has already been exposed to rather rigorous manual systematization; therefore, the addition of the computer is only a new dimension. In other companies the personnel function has few, if any, previous manual systems, and the computer provides a reason for initiating systems. However, companies that try this latter route usually find it an expensive way to proceed. In general, most executives think that it is wiser to decide what systems should be instituted, design them first for manual operation, and then modify them to take advantage of the information capabilities offered by the computer.

As is true of company executives, some personnel managers are much more committed to developing systems than are others. The personnel vice president of a midwestern oil company envisions many things that can be done with systems and seems very eager to get under way. His counterparts in other organizations seem to accept utilization of computers as inevitable, but they are not particularly enthusiastic about the prospect of full-fledged adoption of computers in their own companies. Obviously, these vice presidents will not give wholehearted support if asked to participate in the development of employee information systems.

Previous experience in designing and implementing computer-based systems is very helpful for top personnel executives. They are able to do a much more thorough and concise job of defining for systems people exactly what is wanted or needed. However, few companies have vice presidents of personnel who have been through this process in other organizations. In the one participating company where this was the case, the whole project seems to have proceeded very smoothly. Innovation is a difficult process. When no one has previous experience in developing computer-based employee information systems, both systems people and personnel people feel frustrated about the attempt. Nevertheless, experience is not an absolute necessity; willingness to cooperate is far more important, as pointed out by Quentin Hughes, of Polaroid: "The thing that got us under way was that personnel and systems shared our understanding and worked out compromises. You really have to have both points of view."

Personnel executives who have developed computer-based systems advise: "Don't merely do mechanically what you previously did manually." Gerry Morse, of Honeywell, comments on this: "Using the computer to do what was done before faster and cheaper is to miss the point completely. It has an analogy in the horse and buggy and the automobile. One would be entirely mistaken to think of the automobile as just a faster horse and buggy. Just as the automobile changed the lives of people in our country, emphasizes Mr. Morse, the computer will change the perspective of the personnel function.

One systems manager reports, "Some personnel executives have the attitude that there isn't anything that can be done with computers that can't be done with clerks, if you have enough of them." This may be true for some types of clerical activities, but there are never enough clerks to do all the jobs that can be performed by the computer. Moreover, such an opinion is not conducive to good working relationships between the people in systems and personnel. Personnel should be receptive to learning about possibilities that previously were not feasible and should accept the challenge of designing systems to realize these potentialities rather than feel hurt and defensive because an outsider suggests them. Personnel executives would be wise to heed this statement by Saul Citrone, of IBM: "Today there is no problem with machine technology; we have the equipment to do whatever needs to be done. The problem is in management's inability to define and establish what it wants and needs to do." All managers, not just those in personnel, have to grapple with this problem.

Systems groups, like personnel departments, play different roles and operate in different ways in various companies. Also, systems groups are perceived in different ways by other groups in various companies. In some firms, systems people are perceived as order takers. Because they have operated in a seller's market for so long, they have had more work than they could do with the resources available. As a result, the systems people worked on the projects that were well defined—in which objectives and procedures were fully spelled out—and they provided little assistance for the development of new applications. Thus they neglected departments, such as personnel, that did not recognize the immense possibilities that were available. In such situations the personnel department has been dissatisfied with the overall results of joint efforts.

Personnel executives comment that systems people do not speak the same language as the users of their systems and that they have their own jargon, which is foreign to other people, especially those who have no systems experience. Systems specialists seem to lack interest in translating systems and programming jargon into English or in learning the language of the personnel people.

By the same token, systems specialists voice the same complaint about personnel people. They believe that systems concepts can be expressed only by systems terminology and language. From their point of view, if a person wants to use the services of systems, it is up to him to learn the special words and symbols so that he can communicate. Both groups have defensible positions; therefore, communication problems are reduced considerably when both bend a little. When one refuses to give in to the other, the issue is sometimes sufficient to preclude effective working relationships.

A major complaint of personnel managers is that systems people tend to design mechanically efficient systems, rather than user-effective systems. Systems people point out that they are responsible for designing the best systems possible in line with the definitions provided. In the absence of precise definitions or directives, they usually design mechanically efficient systems.

ORGANIZATIONAL FACTORS

Some managers state that in the past the control of computers in their companies was in the wrong hands. When computer operations and systems design were controlled by a particular area, such as the finance department or the controller's office, they suffered from functional provincialism. Although it is quite natural for the values of such groups to be imposed on the design of all systems that are developed, as several personnel executives have verified, the effects of provincialism are detrimental, both to the department and to the company.

Personnel men in one company report that their systems development was hampered for a long time because computer systems activities were the responsibility of the accounting department. Programs that were developed could get acceptance and budgetary support only if sizable cost savings were demonstrated. Programs that were needed for improving or expanding services but failed to achieve cost savings were discouraged or refused outright. Since only those portions of proposed programs that were demonstrably cost-effective were programmed and implemented, the total systems were, in effect, gerrymandered; thus the system's operations became increasingly inefficient.

Some companies have recognized the problems inherent in having systems and computer operations under the control of a functional division, and they are moving these activities into a separate organizational group that has no responsibilities or ties other than its own special function of providing computer services for the entire organization. For example, at McDonnell Douglas Corporation, in St. Louis, programming assistance and computer services may be purchased from a divisional company, McDonnell Automation Company. In other companies, systems and programming services are now part of user groups, such as the personnel department. These arrangements are not without problems and limitations, but at least they avoid some of the rivalries and value conflicts that have prevailed in companies.

Some systems people are distressed about their organizational position in their companies. Several systems men state that it is time for them to join the management team and develop an interest in the complexities

of management. They express a desire to begin thinking like managers rather than like programmers or systems designers. This transition is important, as Earl Rickheim, of Honeywell, emphasizes: "A systems man must be able to talk knowledgeably with a manager and understand how he manages his operation. When one of my systems men has trouble getting to see a manager, I ask, 'Can you talk intelligently with him about how he manages his operation? If not, why should he take his time to educate you?' "

SUPPORTING SYSTEMS DEVELOPMENT

How are systems usually developed in companies? In some of them, developmental efforts are performed by a team composed of people from systems, functional departments, and other line and staff groups. The teams may be led by systems men or by functional representatives. In some companies line management calls the tune; in others, staff people do. Naturally, the systems developed by these variously composed teams differ considerably. At Honeywell, the corporate personnel department feels strongly that all parties should work closely together, with systems help and support; that the user—the personnel department—should control the design of the program; and that line management should participate fully by serving as a consultant on system design and operation and giving its approval of the design. This opinion is shared by executives in Honeywell's systems group.

In the companies interviewed, top personnel officers give varying degrees of support to systems efforts. In some, personnel executives battle actively to obtain systems and programming assistance; in others, they seek and obtain only a moderate degree of backing. Support is provided for design and programming by insuring an ample budget for computer time, assigning programmers or systems men to the personnel department, and, finally, negotiating at higher levels for adequate support from computer services departments. In some companies, this is a comparatively easy battle because top management has greatly expanded monies available for computer-based systems. In other firms, however, systems activities have expanded very little.

In summary, developing and implementing employee information systems depend to a great extent on organizational factors, top management policies, personnel policies and objectives, and the relationships of people in personnel, systems, and other groups. Although each of these factors influences the personnel department's effectiveness in developing systems, the department is by no means a passive agent in the process. Its strategy and actions not only affect the total developmental process; they are also a major force in determining the success of the company's total systems effort.

Elements of Data Contained in
Personnel Data Banks of Several Companies

PERSONAL DATA

Name	Last
	First
	Middle
Title (Mr., Mrs., Miss)	
Business Address	Street
	City
	State
	Zip Code
Residence	County
	State
	Country
Home Phone	
Social Security Number	
Race	
Sex	
Marital Status	
Age	
Birth	Date
	Place
	Country
Citizenship	Status
	Alien Number
	Date
Personal Data	Effective Date
Office Information	Phone
	Mail Number
	Signature Code
	Check Name
	Joint Tenancy Name
	Spouse Name
Emergency Contact	Name
	Address
	Relationship
	Place of Employment

Record Printout Flag

Military/Reserve-Status	Branch	
	Rank	
	Discharge Type	
	Date	
	Selective Service Classification	
Change-Notice Flag		
Medical Restrictions	Diagnosis	
	Handicap Code	
	Physical Examination Date	
Professional Society	Name	
	Status: Certificate/ Registration Number	
	Year	
	State	
	Company Cost	
Interest in Other Firms		

EDUCATION DATA

High School	Name	
	Course	
	Graduation Year	
College	Name	Code
	Degree or Highest Level	
	Percent Complete	
	Number of Years Attended	
	Major	
	Minor	
	Languages	
	Proficiency	
	Last Year of Contact	

Military Training	School	Status	Effective Date
	Training Type	Workweek Code	
Tuition Aid	School	Union Code	
	Level	Shift	
	Course Identity	Labor Grade or Group	
	Grade	Turnover Type	
	Paid Amount	Seniority Level	Augment Priority
	Date		Date
Record-Change Flag			

Absence History

Declared Hours per Period
Work and Lunch Hours
Weeks Worked, Actual and Possible

SKILLS-INVENTORY DATA

Skill Type		Lost Time	Period to Date
Proficiency (Level)			(PTD)
Experience	Years	Disabling Accidents	
	Type	(Lost Time)	Type
Specialty Development			First Day Out
Effective Date			Time PTD
Preference			Claim Number
Management			Start/Stop Dates
Experience	Type	Leave of Absence	Type
	Years		Leave and Return
	Number of People		Dates
	Amount of Budget	Absence Indicator	Type
Teaching Experience			Total Hours
Patents and Publications			Absent
Security	Level		Paid Hours
	Agency		No Pay Indicator
	Date		Entitled and Paid
	Work Project–		Days/Hours
	Level		Paid Benefits
	Work Area		Nonpaid
Employer Tests	Code		Months Code
	Score		
	Date	*Employee I.D. and Location Numbers*	
	Rating		
			Date
STATUS AND WORK HISTORY DATA		Division (Organization)	
General			Local Division
		Region	
Employee Agreement	Type	Factory or Location Number	
Authorization	Number	Branch	
	Effective Date	Department	
Hire-Transfer-			Personnel Number
Acquisition	Type	Group Classification Number	
	Referral Type	Group	
	Date	Section	
Length of Service		Identification Number	
Adjusted Prior Service		Payroll District Number	

Check Number

Payroll Location

Unit Work Classification
   Number   Effective Date
Department Work
   Classification Number
Job Classification Number
Register Number
Department, Building,
   Floor, Territory
Insurance Contract
   Number   Effective Date
Incentive Group
   Number
Permits (Parcel Pass)
Deposit Account Number
Bank Account Number
Parking Lot Number
Parking Pass Number
Microfilm Frame

Job Number and Titles

Job Title History   Code
                   Level

Occupational Group
Job Number Code   Effective Date
                   Function
                   Application
                   Specialty
                   Time on Position
                   Last Year on
                     Position
                   Foreign Service

Termination/
   Retirement   Type
                   Date

VACATIONS AND OTHER DATA

Vacations

Eligibility Date
Pay Rate
Taken
   and Deferred PTD   Days or Hours
                       Type Code

Future Vacation
   Days or Hours   Indicator

Loan (Time)   Liability Rate $

Sick Leave
Eligibility   Hours
                   Date
Hours Used
Wages Received
Off-Time Hours   PTD
                   Eligibility
                   State Current
                   State Eligibility

Travel Code

Blood Bank Participation

                   Request Dates
                   Blood Type
                   Rh Factor

Receive House Organ

                   Code
                   Effective Date

PERFORMANCE APPRAISAL
Type (Period)   Code
                   Result Code
                   Effective Date

Promotable to———
Promotable Now
Reassignment Code
Next Review Date

RECRUITMENT
(Not same base as other data bank entries.)
Requisition Processing   Requisition
                          Number
                          Date Reporting
                          Name of Applicant
                          In or Out Code
                          Clock Number
                          Job Code
                          Occupational
                            Subgroup
                          Relations Ad-
                          ministrator
                          Date Requisition
                          Received
                          Division
                          Job Title
                          Supervisor

Requisition Processing   Advertising Code

    Department   Effective Date
      Number   Area Code (Phone)
    Staff Administrator   Résumé Routing
    Days Requisition   Type Code
      Open   First Visit
    Transaction   Interview Date
    Error Descriptor   Interview Requested
    Miscellaneous   Interviewers
      Internal Codes   Offer   By
                                            Date
                                            Accepted/Rejected

Applicant Processing

Applicant's Name   Start Date
File Number   Letter to Applicant   Code
Administrator   Requirements   Education Level
Action Code   Major Subject
Current Date   Salary
Source–Agency   Advertisement   Zip Code
                     Cost   Visa
                     Date   Class Standard
                     Résumés Received Skill   Type
                     Media Title   Years

APPENDIX B

Responses to Questions 1 Through 6 in Survey Questionnaire

1. Are you reporting for

Size of Firm	Headquarters	Division Offices	Other	Number of Companies Answering Question
All Firms	92%	8%	—	408
Under 1,000	89%	11%	—	(61)
1,000–5,000	92%	8%	—	(156)
Over 5,000	94%	6%	—	(191)

If you are reporting for headquarters, does your company have divisions?

	Yes	No	
All Firms	85%	15%	403
Under 1,000	67%	33%	(58)
1,000–5,000	83%	17%	(156)
Over 5,000	93%	7%	(189)

Are personnel executives situated at divisions?

	Yes	No	
All Firms	70%	30%	323
Under 1,000	30%	70%	(37)
1,000–5,000	62%	38%	(117)
Over 5,000	85%	15%	(169)

2. Does your company have electronic data processing equipment at—

	Headquarters	Divisions	Both	Neither	Number of Companies Answering Question
All Firms	51%	6%	39%	4%	407
Under 1,000	69%	8%	5%	18%	(60)
1,000–5,000	73%	4%	21%	2%	(156)
Over 5,000	28%	5%	66%	1%	(191)

Are EDP services purchased outside company?

	Yes	No	
All Firms	29%	71%	387
Under 1,000	20%	80%	(60)
1,000–5,000	26%	74%	(146)
Over 5,000	35%	65%	(181)

What type of computer is used at your location?

	Computer	Card Processor Only	
All Firms	96%	4%	368
Under 1,000	86%	14%	(44)
1,000–5,000	95%	5%	(146)
Over 5,000	100%	—	(178)

3. Which EDP applications are presently on the computer at your location? (N=408)

	All Firms	Under 1,000	1,000– 5,000	Over 5,000
Payroll	89%	69%	88%	95%
Accounting	85%	62%	85%	93%
Sales	76%	54%	80%	79%
Inventory	74%	57%	74%	80%
Personnel	66%	48%	58%	79%
Billing	66%	51%	62%	73%
Production	61%	54%	61%	62%
Finance	52%	31%	44%	64%
Engineering	33%	10%	29%	44%
Purchasing	30%	13%	26%	39%
Other	13%	8%	10%	16%

4. If you have personnel applications at your location, where are they processed?

Size of Firm	Entirely at Your Location	At Another Location	At Both	Other	Number of Companies Answering Question
All Firms	78%	5%	17%	—	256
Under 1,000	90%	10%	—	—	(30)
1,000–5,000	92%	5%	3%	—	(86)
Over 5,000	66%	4%	30%	—	(140)

If you have personnel applications at other locations, is the processing at—

	Headquarters	Divisions Only	Both	Other	
All Firms	35%	20%	45%	—	154
Under 1,000	67%	22%	11%	—	(9)
1,000–5,000	51%	23%	26%	—	(43)
Over 5,000	25%	20%	55%	—	(102)

5. If you have personnel applications at your location, how satisfied are you with them?

	Highly	Moderately	Very Little	Not at All	
All Firms	32%	58%	7%	3%	233
Under 1,000	16%	72%	12%	—	(25)
1,000–5,000	36%	56%	5%	3%	(80)
Over 5,000	33%	57%	7%	3%	(128)

6. What changes have occurred in your company?

A. Number of employees in personnel department:

	Increase	Decrease	No Change	
All Firms	9%	10%	81%	233
Under 1,000	—	7%	93%	(30)
1,000–5,000	12%	9%	79%	(81)
Over 5,000	8%	12%	80%	(122)

B. Number of personnel services:

	Increase	Decrease	No Change	Number of Companies Answering Question
All Firms	61%	1%	38%	231
Under 1,000	60%	4%	36%	(28)
1,000–5,000	56%	—	44%	(81)
Over 5,000	64%	1%	35%	(122)

C. Quality of personnel services:

	Increase	Decrease	No Change	
All Firms	68%	3%	29%	230
Under 1,000	54%	7%	39%	(28)
1,000–5,000	67%	—	33%	(79)
Over 5,000	73%	3%	24%	(123)

D. Cost of personnel services:

	Increase	Decrease	No Change	
All Firms	26%	21%	53%	219
Under 1,000	19%	23%	58%	(26)
1,000–5,000	26%	23%	51%	(76)
Over 5,000	27%	20%	53%	(117)

$6.75
BUSINESS

Developing Computer-Based Employee Information Systems

Edward J. Morrison

Today's manpower shortage, government requirements, and rapid turnover make it imperative for management to have more accessible and up-to-date information about their present employees, and even more information about their current and future manpower needs. Now computerized personnel data make it possible. Here is a report that gives you the details of employee information systems, emphasizing their nature and scope and describing the various phases of development and implementation.

You'll find facts on:
- the kinds of data that provide input
- the updating and maintenance of data files
- editing and auditing
- the types of information reported out of the systems
- the use of multiples and other files

Look for information on management and organizational factors that will determine the types of systems selected. Some of these are management attitudes and involvement, the personnel department's objectives and needs, and the system group's position in the organization. Conflicts between departmental values and requirements, changes resulting from computer use, and the degree of company satisfaction are also discussed.

American Management Association, Inc.
135 West 50th Street   New York, N.Y. 10020

Cover design by Jacques Motyl

8144–3099–6